Bloody Valverde

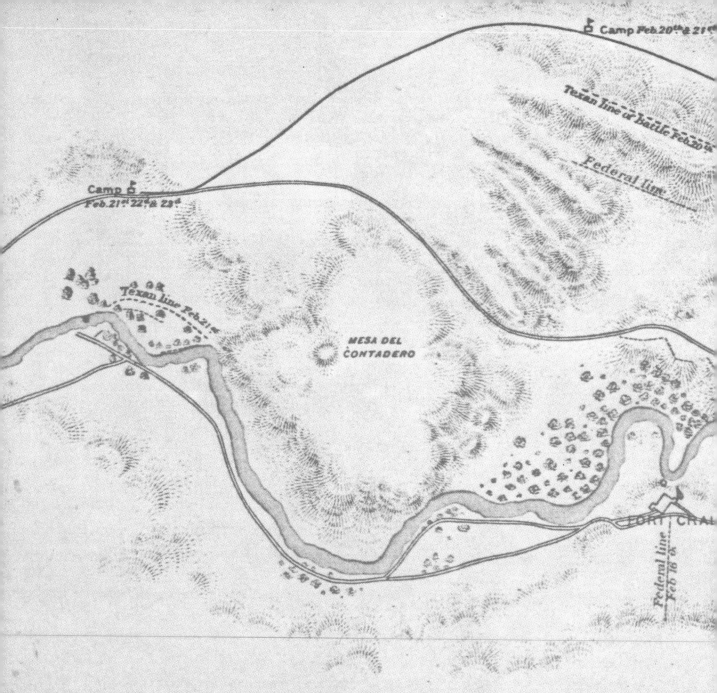

Camp Feb.20th & 21st

Texan line of battle Feb.20th

Federal line

Camp Feb.21st 22d & 23d

Texan line Feb.21st

MESA DEL CONTADERO

FORT CRAIG

Federal line Feb 16 &

OPERATIONS
NEAR
FORT CRAIG, N. MEX.
February, 1862.

Published in cooperation with
the Historical Society of New Mexico

University of New Mexico Press
Albuquerque

Scale

| 1 | 2 | 3 | 4 | 5 miles |

Bloody Valverde

A Civil War Battle
on the Rio Grande,
February 21, 1862

John Taylor

Texan line of Battle Feb 21st

Pa

1.2.3. Texan Camps
Feb. 15th 16th 17th & 18th

Federal line

Library of Congress
Cataloging-in-Publication Data

Taylor, John McLellan, 1947–
Bloody Valverde: a Civil War battle on the
Rio Grande, February 21, 1862 /
John M. Taylor. — 1st ed.
       p. cm.
"Published in cooperation with the
Historical Society of New Mexico."
Includes bibliographical references and
index.
ISBN 0-8263-1632-8 (cl.)
ISBN 0-8263-2148-8 (pbk.)
1. Valverde (N.M.), Battle of, 1862.
I. Title.
E473.4.T38 1995
973.7'31—dc20
94-18763
CIP

Contents

List of Illustrations

List of Maps

Foreword

ON FEBRUARY 21, 1862, SOME 1,700 MILES WEST OF RICHMOND AND Washington, far from the blood-stained fields of Virginia, two American armies clashed in combat beneath a blackened volcanic mesa along the sandy banks of the Rio Grande. Although the men who fought and died at Valverde late in the winter of 1862 were few in comparison to those who waged the legendary campaigns in the East, the stakes in the Southwest were high.

Sharing President Jefferson Davis's concept of a Confederate Manifest Destiny, a grandiose-dreaming and heavy-drinking Brigadier General Henry Hopkins Sibley had raised a brigade of Texans at San Antonio in the late summer of 1861 and marched them west to El Paso and north into the Mesilla Valley. To meet the Rebel Army of New Mexico, Union forces gathered at the adobe bastion of Fort Craig, south of the village of Socorro. The Federals, comprised of frontier Regulars and hastily organized Nuevo Mexicano Territorial Volunteers and Militia, were commanded by the always cautious Colonel Edward Richard Sprigg Canby, who had been with Sibley in Utah and New Mexico before the war. Colonel Canby realized, as did the Texans, that a Rebel victory in New Mexico could open the door to Colorado's mineral-rich Rockies and California's magnificent harbors and gold fields.

Here, for the first time, is a detailed study of the crucial Battle of Valverde—the largest battle ever fought in New Mexico. John Taylor, a nuclear engineer by profession but a historian at heart, provides a perceptive account of this bloody clash of arms.

The reader is certain to enjoy Taylor's portrayal of the major combatants. Present in Union blue were the trail-blazer and Indian agent Colonel Christopher "Kit" Carson at the head of the First New Mexico cavalry; and—perhaps the most courageous of the Federals—Captain Alexander McRae, a North Carolina Unionist who died defending the Federal guns. His body rests at West Point. Captain George N. Bascom, best remembered for his confrontation with Cochise a year earlier at Apache Pass, fell on Valverde's battlefield. Captain Benjamin Wingate lost a leg and died four months later as a result of complications from the amputation. Also in Federal blue was the daring and defiant Irish immigrant—Colonel Canby's eyes and ears—Captain James "Paddy" Graydon, head of his Independent Spy Company.

In the Rebel ranks rode the determined Major Charles L. Pyron and his vanguard of three companies of the Second Texas. One of Sibley's regimental commanders, Lieutenant Colonel William Read "Dirty Shirt" Scurry, survived to lead the Texans at Glorieta later in March, 1862. Colonel Tom Green, a veteran of San Jacinto, ordered the decisive charge of the shotgun-wielding Texans and fell in 1864 at Blair's Landing, Louisiana, while leading an assault on Union gunboats. Major John Schuyler Sutton, a native of New York who had been to New Mexico with the ill-fated Texan Santa Fe Expedition, was shot in the leg at Valverde. He refused amputation and died the day after the battle. Here also is a flashback to another era in the suicidal lancer charge of Captain Willis L. Lang's Company B of the Fifth Texas against Captain Theodore H. Dodd's company of Colorado Volunteers.

The notorious Nicaraguan filibuster, Captain Samuel Lockridge, who bragged that he would make his wife a "shimmy" from the Federal banner flying over Fort Craig, fell in the valiant charge against McRae's battery. And of course General Sibley, a twenty-three-year veteran of the antebellum army, ill, drunk, and unable to command his Confederate Army of New Mexico, nevertheless managed to prove victorious at Valverde.

Besides a thorough use of the *Official Records*, Taylor relies on an impressive array of solidly based primary sources to give us an exciting hour-by-hour narrative of this critical battle. Taylor also compiles and analyzes both Union and Confederate casualties. Moreover, I believe he has resolved exactly what happened around McRae's battery during the pivotal Rebel charge on that fateful wintry afternoon. Taylor also includes a well-researched Order of Battle for both armies, something not available in general studies of the Civil War in the Southwest.

Taylor has written what is certain to be the definitive study of the Battle of Valverde. Historians and general readers alike will enjoy his superb narrative and insightful interpretation.

JERRY THOMPSON
Professor of History
Texas A&M International University

Acknowledgments

MANY PEOPLE HAVE CONTRIBUTED TO THE SUCCESS OF THIS EFFORT. I owe particular thanks to my parents, Clem and Betty Taylor, for instilling in me a love of reading; my Thacher School English teachers, especially David Lavender and Jack Huyler, for instilling in me a love of writing; and the best teacher I ever had, Bill Long, for instilling in me a love of history. I wish to thank Lee and Chris Meyers, Marion Grinstead, Alan Zelicoff, Tom Edrington, Buddy Swingle, Spencer Wilson, and Steve Dupree for their contributions, thorough reviews, and insightful comments. I also particularly recognize the contributions of Dee Brecheisen, New Mexico explorer extraordinaire; Dave Cunnington, master of computer graphics; Don Alberts and Jerry Thompson, true experts on the Civil War in New Mexico and much-appreciated mentors; Chuck Meketa, a collector of papers and a passionate advocate for thoroughness; and Tom O'Brien, a reenactor and writer with "close-to-firsthand" knowledge of Civil War strategy and tactics for their particular contributions.

Finally, this work owes its inspiration and very existence to my wife, Lynn, whose seemingly endless patience, love, and understanding have been and continue to be unsurpassed.

Although the Treaty of Guadalupe Hidalgo ceded ownership of the New Mexico Territory to the United States, it would be many years before the government in "Washington City" exercised significant influence over territorial affairs. For the moment, it made its presence known by assigning about fifteen hundred soldiers to posts in the region. These troops had the challenging job of maintaining order, protecting commerce along the major trade routes, and dealing with the ever-present problem of hostile Indians, across the entire 300,000-square-mile jurisdiction.

By 1861, with war looming in the East, a group of influential New Mexicans, led by Miguel Otero, seriously considered forming a confederation of western territories independent of both Washington and Richmond. This lack of allegiance to either side was not the case in extreme southern New Mexico, especially the Mesilla Valley, where many residents had ethnic, cultural, and economic ties to the South. In fact, on March 3, 1861, a conference in Mesilla declared that the portion of the territory below the Thirty-fourth parallel was no longer a part of the United States but was the "Confederate Territory of Arizona."

So as the clouds of war roiled over the Virginia countryside, the vast majority of New Mexicans struggled with the centuries-old problems of scratching subsistence from the parched caliche soil, unaware, for all intents and purposes, of the momentous events that would soon engulf them.

Most Civil War aficionados familiar with the Confederate invasion of New Mexico will recall the Battle of Glorieta, sometimes referred to as the "Gettysburg of the West," but will note only in passing that there was also an "engagement" at Valverde. Yet this "engagement," which preceded Glorieta by only a month, involved more than twice as many men, caused more than twice the number of casualties, and was instrumental in causing the Confederate army to abandon the field at Glorieta when it did. Moreover, Valverde is arguably a better match for Gettysburg than Glorieta, both tactically and in terms of its ultimate impact. As later chapters will show, Valverde, like Gettysburg, has three distinct phases (albeit over a period of one day versus three). And like Gettysburg in the East, it represented in the West the beginning of the end of any chance that the Confederacy might prevail.

The Confederate incursion into the New Mexico Territory covered about the same distance as that from Gettysburg to Appomattox; and, though no one should argue that the New Mexico campaign equalled in importance the eastern campaigns and battles, the Union might have faced a whole new set of problems had Sibley achieved his overall objectives. According to Trevanion Teel and others, these objectives included the capture of the Colorado goldfields; the annexation of Arizona, Colorado, New Mexico, Utah, Nevada, and perhaps even California; and the incorporation of the Mexican states of Chihuahua and Sonora into the Confederacy.[4] Had Sibley been successful, the outcome of the Civil War might well have been different.

The Battle of Valverde was a tactical victory for the Confederates: Canby and his Union forces had retired from the field in disarray, leaving possession of the ford to Sibley and the Texans. However, the Union forces, though badly bloodied, remained in force astride Sibley's principal line of communication with Mesilla and the rest of the Confederacy; and to leave an enemy force, particularly one as large as your own, at your rear was contrary to military doctrine, not to mention common sense. In addition, the supplies at Fort Craig, one of Sibley's important objectives, remained in Union hands.

These facts lead to speculation that the terrible fighting that took place at Valverde predestined the outcome at Glorieta. The Confederate army lost over two hundred men killed or wounded (including several key officers); they lost hundreds of horses and mules that had drawn their supply wagons and artillery; and they were forced to destroy many of their supplies as a direct result of Valverde.

On the field at Glorieta, late on the afternoon of March 28, 1862, Confederate leaders once again were informed that their supply train was in flames. A few days later, with this logistics catastrophe and the losses at Valverde fresh in his mind and Canby's Fort Craig army nipping at his heels, Sibley's grandiose plan to conquer New Mexico and form a "Western Confederacy" came to an abrupt end as he ordered his army to retreat.

Today Valverde is a marshy, tamarisk-infested river bottom whose stillness is punctuated only by the lowing of an occasional lonely calf and the ever-present buzzing of flies and mosquitos. Major floods inundated the area in 1866, 1884, 1929, and 1939. The railroad arrived in 1880, carving its right-of-way across the western edge of the battlefield. Flood control and irrigation projects, including the construction of Elephant Butte Dam in 1916, changed the watercourse several times, directing it into entirely new channels.[5] Finally, the "invasion" of the tamarisk in the 1930s changed the vegetation pattern, rendering the battlefield virtually unrecognizable from the ground.[6]

However, one distinctive geographic marker, the monolithic Mesa del Contadero, mentioned in official reports by both Union and Confederate officers, stands as a permanent landmark to the battle. Using it, we can approximate the key locations of the fighting on that fateful February day in 1862.[7]

2

Origins

VALVERDE IS TWENTY-FIVE MILES SOUTH OF SOCORRO, NEW MEXICO. The battlefield itself lies in the river bottom four miles southeast of Interstate 25 at the San Marcial exit and about three miles west–southwest of the ruins of the village of Valverde for which the area was named.

In 1862, the field was an alluvial flood plain on the eastern bank of the Rio Grande, punctuated by irregular groves (or *bosques*) of cottonwood trees. The isolated clumps of trees gradually gave way to a sandy slope stretching several hundred yards east through a series of low, north-south sand embankments. These sandy rises delimited an old river channel that turned abruptly east and ran along the north face of Mesa del Contadero. To the south, this mesa rises abruptly from the plain, jutting into the sky some three hundred feet. On the western, northern, and southern faces, the mesa is steep and can be scaled only with some difficulty. To the east, it joins more gradually with the sand-covered lava flows (also called *mal pais* or *pedregal*) that constitute the local highlands.

In 1862, the Rio Grande followed a course slightly west of its present one, beginning a lazy sweep to the west about two miles north of the mesa. Immediately north of the mesa were three fords that had been used by travelers, traders, and Indians for many years.[1]

The village, or *paraje* (stopping place), of Valverde, about three miles upstream from the fords at the northern tip of Mesa del Contadero, may have been occupied off and on since the late 1700s.[2] At the time of the battle, it had about ninety inhabitants. Although it was nearly ten miles north of the Federal military bastion of Fort Craig, Valverde's residents benefited from trade and commerce both with Fort Craig and its short-lived predecessor, Fort Conrad, which had been constructed in the malarial bottomland across from the village.[3]

What brought several thousand men from Texas and New Mexico together at this point on a wintry February day in 1862? Herein lies the tale.

Henry Hopkins Sibley, born in Natchitoches, Louisiana, on May 25, 1816, was a Mexican War veteran and an 1838 graduate of the United States Military Academy at West Point. He was also the inventor of the Sibley tent and Sibley stove, which were popular on both sides during the Civil War. He had served since the early 1850s on the western frontier, most recently assigned to duty at Cantonment Burgwin just south of Ranchos de Taos in north-central New Mexico. For a short time, he served as interim commander of Fort Union, a critical outpost north of Las Vegas, New Mexico, that served both as a quartermaster depot for much of the Southwest and as a staging point for Federal protection of commerce along the westernmost reaches of the Santa Fe Trail.[4]

A charismatic speaker, Sibley possessed a certain charm that had enabled him to compensate for a drinking problem serious enough to earn him the nickname of "the Walking Whiskey Keg."[5] While serving in the West he had been reprimanded and court-martialed but managed to prevail and rise to the rank of brevet major of dragoons.[6]

Like many other army officers in the middle of the nineteenth century, Sibley's political leanings were toward the South. Acting on these sympathies, Sibley submitted a letter resigning his commission on April 28, 1861. When no reply had been received by May 31, he simply packed up and left Fort Union. Meeting some men of the Seventh U.S. Infantry south of Fort Craig, he stuck his head out of the buggy and shouted, "Boys, if you only knew it, I'm [now] the worst enemy you have!"[7]

Sibley rode south, first to El Paso, then on to San Antonio, and finally to Richmond, where in early July he met with Jefferson Davis, persuading him to underwrite a Confederate adventure in the Southwest. Not long after this meeting, rumors of the plan began to filter back to former comrades in New Mexico.

During his presentation to Davis, Sibley no doubt painted a glowing picture—a body of highly mobile, mounted troopers would move west from San Antonio to southern New Mexico where there were already many Southern sympathizers. From there, the force would move up the Rio Grande Valley, capturing the Union's southern bastion at Fort Craig. Resupplied from the stores at Fort Craig, the army would move north along the Rio Grande Valley to occupy Albuquerque and Santa Fe with their important supplies of arms and ammunition. Thus positioned and once again resupplied, Sibley could strike east through Glorieta Pass, eventually overrunning Fort Union itself.

He probably noted that the Military Department of New Mexico was staffed in anticipation of Indian control, not in anticipation of facing determined troops in pitched battle. He would also assert that the territory was staffed by demoralized soldiers and officers, many with latent Southern sympathies.[8] In addition, the Union forces were stretched thin across the territory, charged with protecting its population from Indian depredations.

Once Fort Union was captured and the army had been resupplied, Sibley would move north to the Colorado goldfields. He went on to note that the New Mexican population in general would probably embrace the cause of the Confederacy. In Colorado, too, Sibley assured Davis, they would find substantial Confederate sympathies. Buoyed by these successes and strengthened by volunteer recruits from Colorado, the army would turn west. Utah's Mormon population had no particular love for the Union, so they would be at worst neutral and perhaps even supportive of the Confederate cause. Nevada and California would be next, and once again there they would likely find substantial Southern sympathy.

The pièce de résistance would be a mission to Mexico's northern states of Chihuahua and Sonora. Because of the present turmoil in Mexico, Sibley probably maintained that these states could easily be annexed as the final parts of a "Western Confederacy." And all of this for an initial investment of support for only 3,200 Texans anxious to fight for the South!

It is not surprising that Davis agreed with the plan,[9] for he was encouraged by early southern victories and mindful of the impact on the Union of severing ties with the West and its gold, as well as the impact on potential European allies of such a conquest. He commissioned Sibley as brigadier general in the service of the Confederate States of America and empowered him to raise an army and invade New Mexico.

Southern New Mexico, with its historical trade and kinship ties to the South, had aligned itself with the Confederacy in March of 1861. In July of that year, Confederate Lieutenant Colonel John Robert Baylor and about 400 men of the Second Regiment of Texas Mounted Rifles had been dispatched to lend some military muscle to the prevailing sentiment.

On July 24, 1861, Baylor intimidated Major Isaac Lynde, the incompetent Union commander at Fort Fillmore, into abandoning and firing that post. During an abortive and ill-timed retreat toward Fort Stanton, Lynde and his 500 men were overtaken by Baylor in San Augustin Pass. The Union soldiers struggled in the desert heat, so Baylor simply followed the trail of collapsed and collapsing bluecoats.[10] Lynde felt he had no choice and surrendered his force, the last Union garrison in southern New Mexico, to the Confederates.

General Sibley himself left Richmond in mid-July, and returned to San Antonio. By late October he had formed a 3,200-man brigade of four regiments and trained them sufficiently to declare them ready for battle.[11] On October 21, 1861, the small army, which would become known as Sibley's Brigade, held a grand parade through the narrow streets of San Antonio. Immediately afterward, the vanguard of the expedition, the Seventh Regiment of Texas Mounted Volunteers under the command of Lieutenant Colonel John Schuyler Sutton, marched west for El Paso and points north.

Colonel Edward R. S. Canby, U.S.A., shown after his promotion to major general. Courtesy The Library of Congress.

Colonel Edward Richard Sprigg Canby had taken over command of the United States Military Department of New Mexico on June 11, 1861, from another of the many Southern sympathizers, Colonel William Wing Loring. Canby, too, was a career soldier. Born at Piatt's Landing, Maryland, in 1817 and an 1839 graduate of West Point, he had served in the Mexican War and was twice cited for "gallantry and meritorious conduct."[12]

Canby had served in the West on and off since 1849 and his path and Sibley's had crossed on many occasions. The two officers had served together during the 1857–1858 expedition against Brigham Young and the Mormons. During that campaign, Canby had even served on a court-martial that exonerated Sibley of charges of insubordination. They had also joined forces in the Navajo campaign of 1860.[13]

During June 1861, Canby prepared for the anticipated invasion. Sibley's report to Davis had been correct—the Federal forces were stretched across the more than 300,000 square miles from the Colorado River to the Texas border. Because operations in the eastern U.S. were not going well for the North, officers and men from western garrisons had already been tapped for duty in the East and Canby's pleas for reinforcements fell on deaf ears. Finally, desperate for men and increasingly aware of the threat of a Confederate invasion, military authorities and territorial officials directed Canby to initiate a major recruitment drive, concentrated in northern New Mexico near Santa Fe and Fort Union.

James L. Collins, a former merchant and editor of the "Santa Fe Weekly Gazette" who had been appointed Territorial Superintendent of Indian Affairs by President James Buchanan, noted both the importance of the anticipated confrontation and the reaction of the Hispanic population to recruitment in the face of Confederate rumblings from Mesilla:

> The Mexicans have turned out with a spirit that is truly commendable, the best and most influential Mexicans [in] the territory are here and will take part in the battle. It is an important event in the history of the Territory: if we loose [*sic*] this battle it becomes a part of the Southern Confederacy, at least for a time, and not only that, it [the Territory] will be stripped of its wealth; the property of every man who is known to be favorable to the Gov and they are able, will be robbed and themselves perhaps driven from their homes.[14]

By January 1862, Federal forces in the Territory totalled some 5,500, including about 1,500 regulars and 4,000 volunteers and militia. Although pleased that his numbers had improved, Canby worried about the reliability of the New Mexico Volunteers and Militia in the face of Confederate troops who, by most accounts, were better trained. In particular, while reasonably confident of their ability to defend fortified positions, Canby feared that in a pitched battle, where they might be forced to maneuver under fire, the volunteers would prove inadequate. On the other hand, Territorial Governor Henry Connelly, speaking confidently from the safety of his Santa Fe office, noted:

Territorial Governor Henry
Connelly. Courtesy Museum
of New Mexico, neg. no.
9846.

I have no fears as to the result here. We will conquer the Texan forces,
if not in the first battle, it will be done in the second or subsequent
battles. We will overcome them. The spirit of our people is good, and
I have here and en route 1,000 and more of the elite of the yeomanry of
the country to aid in defending their homes and firesides.[15]

As winter intensified, rumors of the approach of the Confederate
army continued. Lewis Roe recalled:

We were in almost total ignorance of what was going on in the States,
having no mail communication at that time...but we had rumors innu-
merable.[16]

Canby faced a strategic dilemma: there were three major invasion
routes open to Sibley—west along the Canadian River to Fort Union; up
the Pecos River and thence to Fort Union; or up the Rio Grande to Fort
Union by way of Albuquerque, Santa Fe, and Glorieta Pass. Each route
had advantages and disadvantages. But which would Sibley choose? The
Canadian and Pecos routes were shorter and would have fewer points of
opposition, but were sparsely populated and would not permit major
resupply of an army "living off the land." The Rio Grande corridor, though
longer and better defended, offered plentiful water, many villages and

farms, and military installations which, if captured, would resupply the invading force and permit it to "travel light" as it moved up the valley. In any case, Fort Union, the gateway to Colorado and the Santa Fe Trail, was the ultimate objective of the New Mexico phase of Sibley's grand scheme and Canby's crown jewel to be protected at all cost.

Given this strategic situation, Colonel Canby deployed the bulk of his force of volunteers and regulars at Fort Craig. This outpost, established in 1854, was now the southern bastion of Federal forces in New Mexico.[17] He also stationed about 500 men near the town of Belen, about 100 miles north of Fort Craig. From here, troops could theoretically reinforce Fort Craig or move east through Abo Pass (where an advanced company was stationed) to deal with either a Pecos or Canadian River invasion route. In addition, he sent periodic scouting expeditions from Fort Marcy in Santa Fe and Hatch's Ranch (near the confluence of the Pecos and Gallinas rivers) down the Pecos valley.[18] Thus, in mid-January, with Sibley's army trickling into El Paso, Canby's inexperienced forces, still faced with Apache, Kiowa, and Navajo raids across the territory, were readied to deal with the impending Confederate invasion.[19]

In mid-December, 1861, General Sibley issued a proclamation from his headquarters at Fort Bliss to "the people of New Mexico," in which he took possession of the territory for the Confederate States of America and declared his intent to liberate it from the "yoke of military despotism erected by usurpers upon the ruins of the former free institutions of the United States."[20]

On February 7, Sibley finally gave the order and the first units of his army, the Fifth Regiment of Texas Mounted Volunteers under the command of Colonel Tom Green, and Captain Trevanion T. Teel's battery of four six-pounder guns, left Fort Thorn and headed north along the Rio Grande toward Fort Craig and the Union army, some sixty miles away.[21] When word of Sibley's advance reached Canby on February 9, he recalled the rest of the Belen garrison and sent the women of the fort north to Fort Union in anticipation of the inevitable fight.[22] The New Mexico portion of the Civil War had begun in earnest.

3

Prelude to a Fight

By Wednesday, February 12, 1862, Sibley's northbound army stretched over almost sixty miles. Tom Green, a forty-seven-year-old Texas lawyer and Mexican War veteran, commanded the Fifth Regiment. The nearly 930 men of this group, with Teel's artillery in the van, had camped about twenty-four miles south of Fort Craig on the eleventh, laying out the camp in "battle form in two ranks" in anticipation of imminent action.[1]

Green dispatched three companies of the Fifth and a small scouting party under twenty-four-year-old Lieutenant Colonel Henry McNeill to reconnoiter the terrain between the campsite and Fort Craig. The men of the Fifth were led by thirty-three-year-old Major Samuel A. Lockridge, a battle-tested, Alabama-born lawyer who had been seriously wounded in the 1856 Nicaragua expedition.[2]

The rest of the regiment enjoyed pleasant, springlike weather; washed clothes, wrote letters and diaries, and grazed their horses in the river-bottom meadowlands. During the day, Major Charles Pyron, a forty-two-year-old Mexican War veteran from Alabama, led Company B of Baylor's Command and Captain James Crosson's company of the Fourth Regiment (also known as the "Lone Star Rangers") into camp.[3] Green now had a total of about eleven hundred men.

Sibley had lost about five hundred men to smallpox, measles, pneumonia, desertion, and transfer after the brigade left San Antonio. Another, Private William Kemp of Company I of the Fifth, died in camp of pneumonia about noon on the twelfth. He was buried in a campside grave.[4]

The Fourth Regiment of Texas Mounted Volunteers was normally commanded by Colonel James Reily, but that officer had been dispatched to northern Mexico to obtain "security assurances" from the governor

17

Colonel Tom Green, Fifth Texas Mounted Volunteers. Courtesy The Library of Congress.

of Chihuahua. In Reily's absence, command of the 850 men of the Fourth devolved on the regiment's lieutenant colonel, another Texas lawyer—forty-year-old William Read "Dirty Shirt" Scurry. Scurry had already served with distinction during the Mexican War and had been a representative on the 1859 Texas–New Mexico Boundary Commission.[5]

The bulk of Scurry's men camped some twenty-one miles downriver from Green, while Sibley's headquarters detachment remained at Fort Thorn. In fact, on February 12 a train of sutlers from the firm of Grosebecks and Cochran arrived at Fort Thorn and laid out their wares—liquor, preserved fruit, candy, raisins, tobacco, pipes, pipestems, and pants—and the "men of the Regiment reveled in spirits that night."[6]

Wednesday, February 12, 1862, Fort Craig

Anticipation of the approach of the Confederate army heightened the tension at Fort Craig. This garrison, an odd-shaped twenty-acre compound with an external wall and ditch, had been designed to house just two companies of troops and had only recently expanded to add the capacity to deal with a third company, about three hundred men alto-

Lieutenant Colonel William Scurry, Fourth Texas Mounted Volunteers.
Courtesy The Library of Congress.

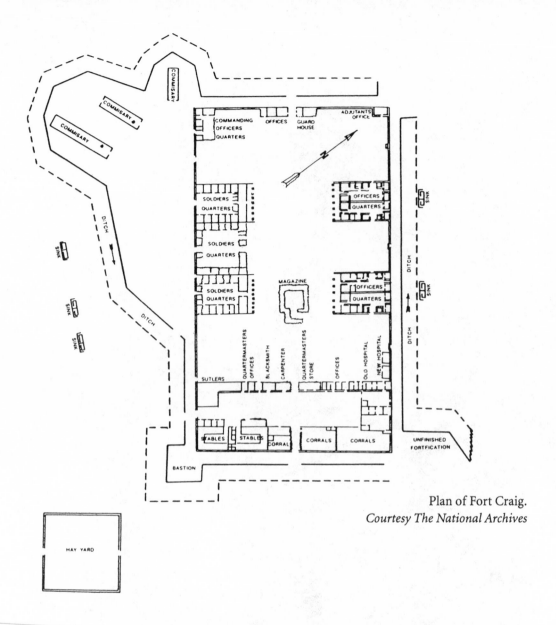

Plan of Fort Craig.
Courtesy The National Archives

gether. The construction was mainly adobe, although there were also structures of stone and some of the wood-lattice "picket-post" design. With the addition of the troops brought south to face the Texans, the post was very crowded.

During the night of the twelfth, Union soldiers were called to arms from their bunks by the "long roll," but they were allowed to return to bed after just a few minutes. In the morning, Captain Rafael Chacón, a twenty-eight-year old officer from a prominent New Mexico family, and his company of First New Mexico Volunteers were dispatched to scout

Fort Craig in the nineteenth century. Courtesy The National Archives.

the west bank of the river, south of the crossing and near the village of Paraje. Chacón divided his force, half of them riding near the river and the other half riding along the escarpment to the west. The two platoons reunited north of the small village of Padercillas (probably near the village of Alamosa) and, having encountered no enemy forces, returned to Fort Craig.

Immediately upon entering the fort, Chacón was ordered to report to Canby. Speaking through an interpreter (since the colonel spoke no Spanish and Chacón no English), he asked if it were true that Chacón and his troopers had been captured and paroled by Confederates that afternoon. Chacón, somewhat taken aback, said that he did not have any idea what Canby was talking about. At that, Captain Charles Deus, assigned to scout the east bank while Chacón was on the west bank, was summoned. He stated that he had spotted two groups of riders coming together on the far side of the river. Unaware of Chacón's division of forces, he had assumed that his compadre had been captured by the Texans, and he so reported to Canby.

Chacón could now appreciate Canby's concern, but his explanation satisfied the nervous colonel and the encounter was closed with a somewhat chagrined Deus being directed to be more careful in his future reports.[7]

On Thursday, February 13, Canby ordered the men of Captain Theodore H. Dodd's company of Colorado Volunteers, together with Captain Benjamin Wingate and Company D of the Fifth U.S. Infantry, to reconnoiter south along the river to Bosque Bonita. After marching for two hours, Federal scouts spotted another of Major Lockridge's Confederate reconnaissance patrols. Immediately, the Union soldiers took up a defensive position in a ravine and dispatched a messenger back to Canby.

When Canby learned that Wingate and Dodd had made contact with what appeared to be a substantial body of the enemy, he called his garrison to arms and most of the three thousand troops moved south to confront the invaders.[8] However, Canby felt that conditions were not right for a pitched battle, so when Lockridge and the Texans retreated from their advanced position he did not pursue.

At 9:00 P.M., informed (erroneously) that the Texans might be attempting to turn his right flank to the west, Canby ordered the force to return to Fort Craig. Arriving at about 11:00 P.M., the troops bedded down, rifles at the ready, anticipating action at any time. Based on information gleaned from some captured "spies," Canby now estimated that Sibley's army numbered about three thousand.[9]

By staging his forces out of Fort Thorn, Sibley had separated his main supply train from the advanced forces under Green and Scurry. Thus, the men of the Fourth and Fifth regiments had little ammunition and were short of blankets and food. H. J. Hunter noted that "if some decisive strike [at Fort Craig] is not made soon, our provisions and clothing will be extremely scant."[10]

The dearth of logistic support was particularly problematic on the thirteenth, when what was to be a two-day storm blew in from the west with cold north winds and driving snow and sleet.

The hungry, cold men of the Fifth, ill-prepared for winter campaigning, struck camp on the morning of the thirteenth and marched twelve miles, arriving at the chosen campsite about twelve miles south of Fort Craig in the early afternoon. In camp less than an hour, they were called to arms by reports of imminent Federal attack. Six companies under Lockridge advanced to meet the "Abs" (a pejorative shortening of "Abolitionists" used by some Confederates), leaving four companies plus Teel's artillery in reserve.[11] The reserve elements formed a line of battle four miles up the valley, but the Federals failed to materialize and the troops returned to camp in the early evening.

Thursday's encounter served only to heighten the anxiety of the already jittery garrison at Fort Craig. On Friday, Canby posted pickets south of the fort, and the Confederate forces drove them in, capturing twenty-one volunteers. Despite this loss, Canby reported to the adjutant general that he had nearly four thousand men and that his New Mexico Volunteers "appeared to be animated by a very good spirit." His men were directed to maintain "three days rations in their haversacks" and to keep ambulances and ammunition wagons "in readiness."[12]

Midnight, Friday, February 14, 1862, Confederate Camp, Thirty-five Miles South of Fort Craig

The men of the Fourth Regiment of Texas Mounted Volunteers, together with five companies of the Seventh, were bugled into the saddle at midnight and headed north. Their track put them in the face of a north wind with sleet and snow "so hard as to almost pull the face off a man."[13] By 8:00 A.M. they reached Green's camp, twelve miles below Fort Craig.

The Texan camp was alive with excitement—the brigade was finally assembled and the Union forces were only a few miles north. Vengeance may have been on the minds of those Texans who had participated in the disastrous invasion of New Mexico in 1842. Others simply may have been glad that the long-awaited confrontation with the Yankees was about to occur. Campfire chatter among the participants in the near encounter between Lockridge and the Federals was that

> men and captains seemed cool and anxious for a fight. Some were cursing the Yankees, some were careless and unconcerned while others were almost praying for an attack.[14]

Later that evening, orders were given to cook rations for twenty-four hours and to be prepared to march before sunrise. Hanna noted that "the men were ready for a big fight or a foot race."[15]

Although all of the troops were now together, the wagon train still had not caught up with the main column, so after their animals were picketed and their rations prepared, the troops of the Sibley Brigade spent another miserable night with little food and no blankets in the chill of a New Mexico winter.

These Texans were all in the same army but an outside observer would hardly have known so from their appearance. They had shoes and boots of all types, socks of all colors, either gray woolen or woolen plaid jeans, single- or double-breasted coats, and headgear that ranged from wide-brimmed brown or black felt hats to simple colored handkerchiefs.[16]

Saturday dawned with a significant improvement in the weather. The Fifth and Seventh Regiments and the men of Baylor's Command broke camp early and marched upriver for several hours, following the roadway on the western riverbank. Scouts and outriders roamed ahead of the column and on its flanks, ever alert for their Federal counterparts who occasionally could be seen galloping off from observation points on the highlands or across the Rio Grande.

Midway through the afternoon, the Confederate column came to a stretch of riverbank where three large arroyos (Simons, Sheep, and Lumbre canyons) empty into the river from the northwest. The mouths of these arroyos were broad, open expanses with some forage for the animals and plenty of room for the brigade. The Texans set up campsites on the northern and southern edges of the northernmost of these arroyos (Simons Canyon).

Pickets were stationed to the north and west of the campsites, and those assigned to the high ground to the west caught their first glimpse of Fort Craig, four miles to the north. Even through field glasses, details of the fort's activities were difficult to discern; however, there was no mistaking the Stars and Stripes fluttering in the afternoon breeze. Here the Texans saw their first major military objective, although the adobe walls and extent of the fortifications must have given them pause.[17] Confederate lookouts and forward pickets may also have spotted the arrival of the lightly guarded seventy-wagon supply train, which arrived at the fort on the fifteenth with much-needed food for Canby's garrison.[18]

Sunrise, Sunday, February 16, 1862, Confederate Camp South of Fort Craig

After making camp on Saturday night, Sibley and his commanders decided to test Canby's resolve by making a "reconnaissance in force" against the southern face of the fort. The terrain here, broad and relatively flat, favored an open fight. Sibley recognized the potential of a strong, semi-concealed Confederate defensive position in the arroyo to the south. In addition, although the high ground to the west was out of artillery range of the fort, the Confederates could use this terrain feature to bombard Federal lines drawn up on the plain in front.

Sibley probably had confirmed from the captured soldiers that the lion's share of the Federal forces at the fort were New Mexico Volunteers and Militia. He may even have shared Canby's opinion of the fortitude of these inexperienced and untested troops—although his years in New Mexico should have left no doubt in his mind about the prevailing anti-Texas sentiment of a population that disciplined its children by threatening, "If you are not good, I'll give you to the Tejanos, who are coming back!"[19]

Many of the Texans were confident that there wouldn't be much of a fight. Major Lockridge bragged that

> he would make his wife a shimmy out of the [Union] flag and that if he could get a wife as easy as he would get the flag, he will never sleep by himself anymore![20]

UNION ORDER OF BATTLE

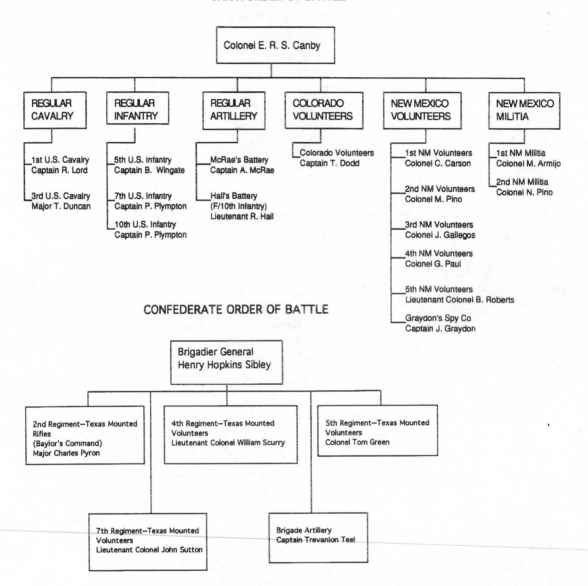

Colonel E. R. S. Canby

REGULAR CAVALRY	REGULAR INFANTRY	REGULAR ARTILLERY	COLORADO VOLUNTEERS	NEW MEXICO VOLUNTEERS	NEW MEXICO MILITIA

REGULAR CAVALRY
- 1st U.S. Cavalry Captain R. Lord
- 3rd U.S. Cavalry Major T. Duncan

REGULAR INFANTRY
- 5th U.S. Infantry Captain B. Wingate
- 7th U.S. Infantry Captain P. Plympton
- 10th U.S. Infantry Captain P. Plympton

REGULAR ARTILLERY
- McRae's Battery Captain A. McRae
- Hall's Battery (F/10th Infantry) Lieutenant R. Hall

COLORADO VOLUNTEERS
- Colorado Volunteers Captain T. Dodd

NEW MEXICO VOLUNTEERS
- 1st NM Volunteers Colonel C. Carson
- 2nd NM Volunteers Colonel M. Pino
- 3rd NM Volunteers Colonel J. Gallegos
- 4th NM Volunteers Colonel G. Paul
- 5th NM Volunteers Lieutenant Colonel B. Roberts
- Graydon's Spy Co Captain J. Graydon

NEW MEXICO MILITIA
- 1st NM Militia Colonel M. Armijo
- 2nd NM Militia Colonel N. Pino

CONFEDERATE ORDER OF BATTLE

Brigadier General Henry Hopkins Sibley

- 2nd Regiment—Texas Mounted Rifles (Baylor's Command) Major Charles Pyron
- 4th Regiment—Texas Mounted Volunteers Lieutenant Colonel William Scurry
- 5th Regiment—Texas Mounted Volunteers Colonel Tom Green
- 7th Regiment—Texas Mounted Volunteers Lieutenant Colonel John Sutton
- Brigade Artillery Captain Trevanion Teel

The Rebels broke camp and formed a line of battle approximately one-half mile long, with their right flank anchored on the riverbank and their left on the high ground to the west. The artillery and several hundred sharpshooters were placed in reserve. In this alignment, they began to advance toward the fort.

4

Opening Gambits

Monday, Tuesday, February 17 and 18, 1862, Confederate Camps Four Miles South of Fort Craig

THE ALMOST-FIGHT ON THE SIXTEENTH HAD BEEN A TRUE BAPTISM OF fire for only a few. However, the minor encounter confirmed Sibley's suspicions that it would be ill advised to attack Fort Craig in a frontal assault. The Federals had a 1.3:1 numerical advantage. Moreover, they enjoyed an advantage in artillery (although Canby had fewer cannons, they were of a higher quality than Sibley's) as well as the defensive advantage of the fort's adobe walls and outlying ditch.

So, while most of the Texans rested in riverbank campsites south of Fort Craig and tried to protect themselves from one of New Mexico's ferocious dust storms, Sibley and his regimental commanders formulated an alternate plan. Meanwhile, Company I of the Fifth Texas Mounted Volunteers, under Captain Ira Killough, and Company D, under Dan Ragsdale, were sent out to watch the fort to ensure that Canby, too, was waiting out the storm.[1]

If Fort Craig could not be taken by assault, perhaps the Texans could draw Canby and his forces into the open, where they could divide the Federal army and defeat it piecemeal. After poring over the maps and scouting the area, Sibley decided to move two miles south of his campsite to the ford near Paraje de Fra Cristobal, or simply Paraje.[2] Crossing the Rio Grande and turning north on the eastern shore, they would skirt the eastern edge of Mesa del Contadero and move to control the critical ford at Valverde, seven miles north of Fort Craig. In this way, Sibley hoped to draw Canby from his defensive bastion.

Thus, at least initially, the odds would be far better for the Texans. However, Sibley must have realized that, in view of his deteriorating logistical situation, both the risk and potential consequences of a less-than-decisive Confederate victory were high.

Considering the previous day's engagement, even with so few casualties and in light of consistent reconnaissance reports, Canby now knew that he faced a significant enemy force. Although he had been receiving regular reports on Sibley's progress north from Fort Thorn, this was his first reliable assessment of the entire Confederate army. So, as Sibley planned his circuitous route to Valverde, Canby once again sent Graydon out to watch the Texans. Meanwhile, he pondered the situation: Would Sibley try to attack the fort again, this time from the east? Would he move to Valverde and cut off Fort Craig by capturing the all-important ford? How would the New Mexico Volunteers and Militia perform when the real fighting began?

If Alonzo Ickis is to be believed, Canby probably shared few of these thoughts and concerns, even with his highest-ranking officers:

> Many rumors afloat as the enemy is near but we know not of the course to be pursued whether we will go out and meet the enemy or wait for them to attack the Fort. Canby counsels none. If Colonel Roberts would ask him what he was going to do, Canby would say, "When 'Boots and Saddles' blows you will know and I'll expect you to be ready to strike!"[3]

On the night of the seventeenth, Fort Craig's silence was broken by a series of gunshots, and the men were again roused from their blankets and ordered into formation by the long roll. A quick check revealed nothing more than a drunken soldier firing off a few pistol rounds. The men returned to their beds, as anxious as ever.[4]

Wednesday, February 19, 1862, On the Western Bank of the Rio Grande, Four Miles South of Fort Craig

The Confederate forces broke camp early and started across the river at the ford northwest of Paraje de Fra Cristobal. This village was built near one of the few breaks through the sand-covered lava flows on the eastern shore. This gap provided access for wagons and travelers between the ford and the trail that ran along the mesa, a mile or so east of the river.

The crossing was cold, but leisurely, with plenty of time to water the horses, mules, and "beeves" (cattle) and to fill canteens. The caravan then had a short three-mile march southeast toward Paraje. Most of the village's two hundred residents had fled when the "Tejanos" came up the river. Maximiano Madril, a boy of about ten in 1862, later recalled that his mother kept him in the house when the Confederates approached the village. Camp was established outside the village about 3:00 P.M. on the nineteenth.[5] Before bedding down (with their weapons at the ready), the Confederates were ordered to cook three days' rations and to be prepared to rise at first light and march north to battle.

Union scouts carefully monitored the movement of the Texans. At about 4:00 A.M., Canby ordered Captain Henry Selden's battalion, plus New Mexico Mounted Volunteers under Lieutenant Colonel José Valdez and the renowned scout and Indian fighter Colonel Christopher "Kit" Carson, to cross the river and occupy the high ground across from the fort. That afternoon, the five recently arrived companies of the Second New Mexico Militia under Colonel Nicholas Pino were also added to Canby's east-bank contingent across from Fort Craig. Having secured the heights unopposed, they made no effort to move south into a position from which they could engage the enemy now camped at Paraje. Anticipating the possibility of a Texan attack, Canby directed the force to remain on the dry, windswept bluff throughout the night.[6]

Some troops under Chacón also moved. Warily, they rode south along the west bank to the now-abandoned Confederate campsites in Simon's Canyon, where they found fresh graves that they reported erroneously as Rebel casualties from the skirmishing on the sixteenth.[7]

February 20, 1862, Paraje de Fra Cristobal

In the cold pre-dawn, Sibley struck camp and headed north. He divided the brigade into two parts. Captain George Milton Frazier, an "Arizona Ranger" familiar with the Fort Craig environs, took the lead with half the command. Sibley placed the wagon train in the center, with the remainder of the command bringing up the rear.

After marching four miles, the lead units crested a small rise and could see Fort Craig four miles to the north, on the bluffs across the river. Seeking to avoid closing within range of federal artillery, Sibley ordered his column to turn on a right oblique and the brigade moved northeast up an arroyo toward higher ground.[8]

As they moved off the hard-packed trail, the Texans encountered deep sand in the arroyo bottom. Wagons and artillery sank to their hubs. Soldiers struggled and swore as they put their shoulders to the heavy wagons, inching them slowly upward toward the higher ground.[9]

The final mounted company of the Second New Mexico Militia arrived at Fort Craig on the twentieth, filling out the regiment of six companies organized under Colonel Pino and Lieutenant Colonel Jesús María Baca y Salazar.[10] Despite rumors of more militiamen nearby, commanded by O. P. Hovey, these would be the last "reinforcements" to reach Canby before the battle. Henceforth, he and the thirty-eight hundred men of his command would be on their own.

Plan of Army operations near Fort Craig as presented in Canby's after-action report.[11]

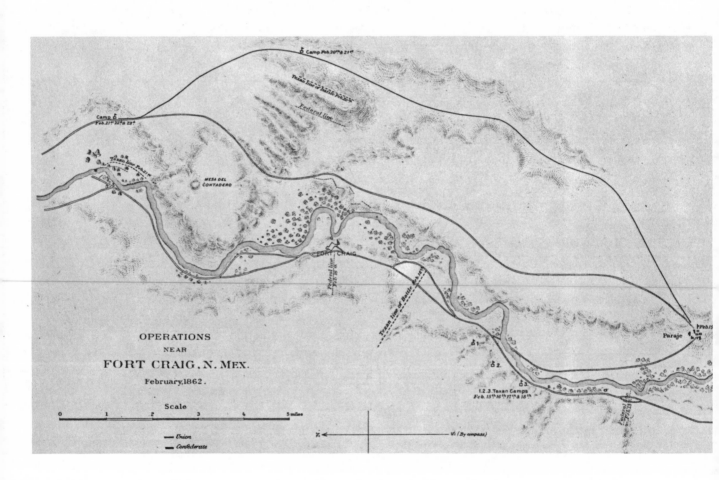

Canby had decided to take the fight to Sibley. He left the fort about two in the afternoon and crossed the river with the remainder of his infantry, cavalry, and McRae's artillery. Once across, they were joined by Carson, Selden, and Pino, who moved back from their overnight position on the bluff.[12]

The march from Paraje had been rough and dry, perhaps reminiscent for some of the Texans of the last part of the trek from San Antonio to El Paso. For several hours, outriders on Sibley's left flank had been reporting on the movement of Federal troops. First, cavalry had appeared on a ridgeline to their north. Then, infantry became visible to the northwest, crossing the river below Fort Craig and struggling up the sandy ravines that led east from the river to the heights. It was clear to Sibley, Green, and the others that their line of advance and Canby's would converge about three miles south of the mesa.

Hoping to engage Canby's forces while the Texans still retained control of the heights and while there was still enough daylight to fire effectively on the Federals below, Sibley put the men of his advanced group in line of battle on the ridgeline. Meanwhile, in the ravine behind him, teamsters and soldiers continued to struggle with wagons in the deep arroyo sand.

As the Fifth Regiment's small brass band struck up "Dixie" and the regimental battle flags were unfurled, artillerymen of the Fourth and Fifth Regiments readied their twelve-pounder mountain howitzers. Captain Trevanion Teel's men unlimbered their four six-pounder guns in the center of the line of battle, trained them to the northwest on the struggling Federals below, and awaited the order to fire. They did not have long to wait—Tom Green, acting on behalf of Sibley (who was, by his own admission, "confined to his ambulance" and probably drunk), ordered Teel to open fire. The six-pounders boomed to the northwest as the Confederates cheered.[13]

Before leaving the fort, Canby ordered a contingent of about six hundred cavalrymen from the First and Second New Mexico Volunteers—probably including First Lieutenant Saturnino Baca, a future adversary of Billy the Kid in the infamous Lincoln County wars—to reoccupy the high ground due east of the fort. Chacón's company, along with the other troopers,

Captain Trevanion Teel, Second Texas Mounted Rifles. Courtesy Archives Division, Texas State Library.

reached a ridgeline about a mile southeast of Mesa del Contadero after a sandy two-hour uphill struggle. Here they had a clear view of the ridgeline to the south, where the rebels were forming a line of battle—cavalry and infantry with artillery in the center.[14]

Immediately, Canby dispatched a detachment of infantry and cavalry to Chacón's right. They, too, struggled eastward and upward through the sandy ravines.[15] He ordered skirmishers from the Seventh U. S. Infantry and from Colonel Miguel Pino's Second Regiment of New Mexico Volunteers forward to a position about eight hundred yards from the Confederate's ridgeline position, to draw the Texan's fire so that their deployment, particularly their battery locations, could be confirmed. Suddenly, with the strains of a brass band drifting overhead, a series of explosions shattered the late afternoon shadows.[16]

Although Chacón's men were "in a position that their [cannon] balls could not touch," two of the New Mexico Volunteers (Tomás De La O of Captain Francisco Abreu's company and a soldier of Captain Saturnino Barrientos's company) were slightly injured by flying rocks and shrap-

Lieutenant Colonel Benjamin S. Roberts, Fifth NM Volunteers, shown after promotion to major general. Courtesy Massachusetts Commandery, Military Order of the Loyal Legion and the U. S. Army Military History Institute.

nel. For the volunteers and militiamen in the arroyo, the Confederate cannonade was also a most unwelcome turn of events. Some of the men had been mustered in as recently as January 1862 and had barely become acquainted with their weapons, much less become seasoned enough to be unmoved by a confrontation with the working end of a Confederate cannon. As Teel's rounds exploded on the hillsides, showering the men with rocks and fragments, some of Pino's men cowered, then broke and ran.[17] Hugh Brown, the youngest man in the Colorado Volunteers, was also hit by an artillery round and mortally wounded.[18]

Lieutenant Colonel Benjamin Stone Roberts, a fifty-one-year old, combat-hardened West Pointer (class of 1835), was in command of the Federal cavalry supporting Canby's afternoon assault. Roberts was a Vermonter, from a family with an illustrious military background. He was a soldier, a lawyer, an engineer, and an inventor, and he had been the chief engineer of the Champlain and Ogdensberg Railroad, as well as geologist for the state of New York. In 1842 he had assisted George Washington Whistler in the construction of the Moscow-to-St. Petersburg railroad in eastern Russia. In addition, he was twice breveted during the Mexican War and had served on the frontier since the end of that conflict.[19]

Aware of his disadvantageous position, and with a significant portion of his force now in retreat, Canby ordered Roberts to make a forceful demonstration with a large contingent of Union cavalry on the Confederate right. Under this cover, the remainder of the force disengaged and the tired, cold, demoralized troops moved back down the hill to a protected perimeter on the riverbank. Some of the volunteer infantry remained overnight on the high ground just south of the mesa to prevent placement of Rebel artillery in a position from which the Texans could shell the fort. In addition, some of the Federal infantry remained in the fortified entrenchments near the river on the eastern bank to protect access to the ford below Fort Craig.[20]

The remainder of the Federals waded back across the river and climbed the bluff to the fort. The regular garrison bedded down in their quarters, while most of the volunteers and militia returned to their campsites outside the walls.[21]

As the sun disappeared behind the western mountains, the Confederates pitched camp on the sandy highlands behind the bluff they had just defended. Tents were set up among the sage and mesquite. They were probably laid out roughly according to Army Regulations, and based on later occurrences, it seems likely that the Fourth Regiment was the westernmost unit.[22]

Pickets were posted, videttes dispatched, and some of the tired Confederates munched on cold bread and dried beef. Others scrounged a few scraps of mesquite from the mesa and made cooking fires. They no doubt heated some of their precious water for coffee and perhaps cooked some "hot dogers," wet dough biscuits cooked over hot embers, to go with the dry jerky. They also used the fires to melt lead and cast bullets, then bedded down as best they could. Deriving what little satisfaction they could from their late afternoon success, they attempted to ignore the cold and their thirst.[23]

Soon after nightfall, Sibley had his bugler sound "Officers' Call." When the officers had gathered, they discussed the day's activities and formulated a plan for the next day. Sibley intended to send Sutton and Green, with Teel's artillery and a sizable force from the Fifth and Seventh regiments, to threaten the fort from the eastern bluffs, while he personally led the remainder of the brigade north around the mesa to the ford at Valverde. The officers coordinated plans, made one last check of their troops, then stretched out to get some rest before the action they all anticipated. There may even have been a "pep talk" or two. Charles Scott of the Fifth Texas Mounted Volunteers reported that Colonel Green told his men, "Boys, you've come too far from home hunting a fight to lose—you must win tomorrow or die on the battlefield."[24]

Evening, February 20, 1862, Union Lines below the Confederate Camp

Allegedly with Colonel Canby's blessing, Paddy Graydon and a few select men from his "spy company" had secured two old mules and a dozen or so twenty-four-pounder artillery shells from the Fort Craig armory. They put the shells into wooden panniers, cut the fuses, and lashed the panniers to the backs of the mules. Crossing the river just below the fort in the early evening and passing through the Union lines, Graydon and his small force slunk southeast across the sandy ravines and pedregal, hoping that the braying of the thirsty Confederate mules— most of which had not been watered for twenty-four hours—would muffle their approach and distract the Texans' pickets. Late in the evening, Graydon and his "spies" drew within a few hundred yards of the Confederate camp.

The Texans had picketed their horses and pack mules by regiment, and those of the Fourth Regiment were closest to Graydon's position. Checking the panniers one more time and cinching the straps another notch for good measure, Graydon lit the fuses and, with a sudden yell and waving of hats, drove the mules toward the Confederate camp.

Now, whether Graydon's mules perceived some sort of Dantesque vision from the few isolated fires, the strange night shadows, and the braying strangers, or whether they simply heard a few shots from the now-aroused Confederate pickets, they decided rather "to bear those ills they knew than to flee to others that they knew not of," and they turned back toward Graydon and his scouts. Finding themselves on the horns of a dilemma, the Federals leapt upon their horses and galloped west down the ravine, no doubt hoping (and praying) that the fuses' time delays were not too long (and probably cursing the leader who had gotten them into such a quandary). Fortunately for Graydon, though not for the two "volunteer" mules, the charges detonated before the mules could catch up with the fleeing Federals.[25]

This entire commotion may have been too much for some of Sibley's Fourth Regiment mules, which were apparently rather poorly secured to begin with. About 150 of them, either frightened by Graydon's shells or simply overwhelmed by thirst, proceeded to stampede toward the river where they were allowed to quench their thirst before being dutifully rounded up by the light of the waning moon and taken to Fort Craig by the Federal pickets guarding the river bottom.[26]

5

The Battle Is Joined

5:30 A.M., February 21, 1862, Confederate Camp
East of Mesa del Contadero

BECAUSE OF THE OPEN ANIMOSITY BETWEEN BAYLOR AND SIBLEY, Major Charles Pyron had been placed in command of the detachment of the Second Texas Mounted Rifles, known as "Baylor's Command," during the invasion of New Mexico. Baylor himself was occupied in governing Confederate Arizona and chasing Apaches in the south. At Sibley's direction, Pyron left the Confederate camp before sunrise with orders to scout the trail around Mesa del Contadero to the ford. He proceeded north with 180 men of Companies B (Lieutenant William Jett), D (Captain James Walker), E (Captain Ike Stafford), and the San Elizaro Spy company (Lieutenant Lemuel Nicholson).[1]

Because the trail was sandy and the horses were thirsty, the troopers moved relatively slowly behind the mesa in a column of fours. Passing about a quarter-mile east of the east face of Mesa del Contadero, they arrived at the northwest edge of the mesa overlooking the ford in about an hour. Although the morning was cold and cloudy, some alert Texans may have noticed a faint reddish-tinged morning star just above Sagittarius in the southeastern sky. Mars, the god of war, was also up early this February day.[2]

Pyron stopped and surveyed the river bottom, about a mile distant in the still darkened valley. Seeing no sign of Federal forces, he sent a message to Scurry reporting that the ford was clear. He then ordered his men down the steep arroyo. The troops proceeded at a leisurely pace to the edge of the treeline, where they turned slightly to the north for a few hundred yards to the upper ford. Reaching the upper ford, they watered their thirsty horses.[3]

Meanwhile, a "very weak" Sibley, still suffering from his Jim Barleycorn–induced "illness" and reluctantly astride his horse, ordered the rest of the brigade to break camp. Discovering the loss of the Fourth Regiment's mules, he modified his plan. Instead of having Green and Sutton threaten the fort from the east, he ordered the column to follow Pyron to the ford. The Fourth's wagonmaster was dispatched to search for the mules,[4] and about thirty of the now-immobile wagons were off-loaded and some of the blankets, books, ammunition, papers, and camp utensils were abandoned. The remainder of the train was repacked and formed in a line of march to the north, with Scurry's Fourth Regiment of Texas Mounted Volunteers in the van.[5]

Canby's pickets and scouts were strung along the river and atop the mesa with orders to "watch the movements of the enemy, threaten his flanks and rear, and impede his movements as much as possible."[6] When the Confederates began their pre-dawn march north, the word was quickly relayed to Fort Craig. Armed with this information, Canby decided to send a mixed battalion of infantry, cavalry, and artillery to the Valverde ford. Lieutenant Colonel Roberts was dispatched with Major Thomas Duncan's cavalry;[7] four mounted companies from the Third New Mexico Volunteers under Lieutenant Colonel José Valdez,[8] Captain Alexander McRae and two of the three sections of his light battery,[9] Lieutenant Robert H. Hall and his battery of two twenty-four-pounder field howitzers, and several companies of infantry,[10] for a total of about 850 men and six cannons (see Appendix).

As they left the fort, Roberts directed Duncan to leave one company of troopers with the infantry column[11] and to proceed rapidly with the other four to the northern end of the mesa to prevent the Confederates from obtaining a lodgement at the ford.[12]

The cavalry units commanded by Chacón and Graydon, leading Duncan's cavalry, reached the northern end of the mesa at about 6:45 A.M. and crossed at the lower ford "just as we were able to see the sun behind the hills".[13]

Shortly after fording the icy Rio Grande, Union pickets spotted Pyron's Confederates moving northwest beyond the treeline toward the upper ford. Word was sent to Duncan, still on the west bank, who dispatched Vermont-born Lieutenant Ira Claflin, leading Company G of the First U.S. Cavalry, to ride north along the west bank to monitor the

Major Thomas Duncan, Third U.S. Cavalry, shown after promotion to colonel. Courtesy Massachusetts Commandery, Military Order of the Loyal Legion and the U.S. Army Military History Institute.

Lieutenant Robert Hall, Tenth U.S. Infantry, shown after promotion to brigadier general during the Spanish American War. Courtesy Massachusetts Commandery, Military Order of the Loyal Legion and the U.S. Army Military History Institute.

movements of the Confederates. It took Claflin only a few minutes to spot Pyron's battalion watering their horses about three-fourths of a mile upriver and to report this to Major Duncan, anxiously waiting at the lower ford.

6:30 A.M., February 21, 1862, East Bank below Fort Craig

In addition to the forces sent north to Valverde, Canby ordered Major Charles Emil Wesche of the Second New Mexico Militia, an attaché on the staff of Territorial Governor Henry Connelly,[14] to reinforce the defensive position on the eastern bank of the river across from Fort Craig, along the southwestern edge of Mesa del Contadero. Wesche and 108 men, under Captains Ramón Sena y Rivera and José Sanchez, crossed at the ford below the fort and set up a defensive position. Immediately to the south was the main Federal position held by Captain Henry R. Selden and his 670-man infantry battalion; the First New Mexico Volunteers, under Colonel Carson (reduced to about 460 men since Rafael Chacón's company had gone to the ford with Duncan); and Colonel Nicholas Pino's detachment of militia (about 200 men). The latter two battalions had operated in that area since the nineteenth or twentieth.

7:30 A.M., February 21, 1862, Upper Ford—East Bank

The Confederate cavalry battalion under Pyron reached the heavy stand of cottonwoods that lined the eastern riverbank between 7 and 7:30. Quickly, they watered the thirsty horses and filled their canteens.

As they turned back to rejoin the main column, however, outriders spotted Union cavalry several hundred yards downstream in the woods on their right. Sensing that he had at least a temporary numerical advantage, Pyron quickly dispatched Captain John Phillips, forty-one-year old leader of the unique group of scouts called "The Brigands,"[15] to notify Sibley of his impending engagement, and then ordered an attack. The 180 Confederate troopers wheeled to the south, driving the 100 or so Federal skirmishers toward the lower ford with a "substantial discharge from their carbines which lasted about an hour."[16]

Lieutenant Colonel Scurry, initially unaware of Pyron's early morning move to the ford, had also established the eight-hundred-man Fourth Regiment in a line of march toward Valverde. Captain Frazier and his "Arizona Rangers" acted as guides, and four companies under thirty-five-year-old Major Henry W. Raguet were sent ahead.[17] Raguet was a wealthy, thirty-six-year-old merchant from Nacogdoches, Texas, who has been described as "blonde, upward of 6 feet, athletic, and affable." He had joined the Fourth Texas Volunteers as the captain of Company H in June 1861.[18]

Patrols from Frazier's company scouted the front and flanks in an attempt to detect any Union threat. One section of Teel's battery, two six-pounders under the command of Lieutenant James Bradford, was placed at the front of the column with Scurry's regiment. Teel himself, as well as his other two guns, remained near the rear of the column.[19]

Major Charles Wesche, Second NM Militia. Photo by James N. Furlong, courtesy Museum of New Mexico, neg. no. 13121.

Colonel Christopher "Kit" Carson, First NM Volunteers. Courtesy The Library of Congress.

The four hundred men of the Seventh Regiment, led by Lieutenant Colonel Sutton, moved out with the train.

Colonel Green held the 840-man Fifth Regiment in reserve at the campsite in the hope that Canby might continue to worry about the possibility of a direct attack on Fort Craig from the east or south and hold some forces at the fort. In addition, they safeguarded the all-important beef herd, so critical to Sibley's logistical strategy.

The deep sand that had slowed Pyron's troopers also slowed the wagons and the thin-wheeled artillery accompanying Scurry and Sutton. The wagonmasters and artillerymen were ordered to dump all unnecessary equipment to lighten the loads as they struggled to move the cannons and wagons across the sandy highlands behind the mesa.

When he was informed that Sibley had dispatched Pyron to the ford ahead of him, Scurry recalled Raguet to the front of the main column. Because the regiment was now strung out and separated, Scurry welcomed Pyron's report that the way was clear. Now the brigade could proceed to the ford unimpeded, and both man and beast could get a long-awaited drink. Unfortunately for the men of the Fourth Texas, this relief was short-lived.

Captain Phillips galloped up at about 8:30 with the news of Pyron's initial engagement in the bosque. Scurry immediately ordered Raguet and his four companies, as well as the Fourth Regiment's artillery under Lieutenant John Reily, the twenty-six-year-old son of the regiment's absent commanding officer, to accompany him to Pyron's aid on the double.

8:00 A.M., February 21, 1862, Union Cavalry at the Lower Ford

The Union's Major Duncan received Claflin's report at almost the same time as he heard the first shots ring out across the river. Aware of the strategic value of the heavy stand of cottonwoods on the eastern shore in controlling the lower ford, he sent a courier back to notify Roberts and immediately ordered the five companies of troopers, under battalion command of Captain Robert Morris, plus the three companies of New Mexico cavalrymen under command of Lieutenant Colonel Valdez (a total of about 480 men) to cross the river, dismount, join Chacón and Graydon and move forward into the bosque as skirmishers.[20]

Duncan's skirmishers opened a brisk fire on Pyron's battalion as the men moved downstream. Soon, Pyron's men were forced to veer to the east side of the bosque. They took cover behind the westernmost of the sand embankments that formed the edge of the old riverbank below the north edge of the mesa, some seven hundred yards from the river itself.[21]

As the Texans established themselves behind the embankment, Duncan formed a strong skirmish line of about 360 dismounted troopers between the lower and middle fords. He ordered the other 120 men to hold the battalion's horses in a semiprotected area behind the battle and east of the riverbank.

The Federal skirmishers were armed with long-range rifled muskets and minié balls.[22] Most of the regulars had Model 1855 .58 caliber rifled muskets. The New Mexico Volunteers generally had Model 1841

.54 caliber weapons known as Mississippi Rifles or .69 caliber smooth-bore muskets that had been altered from flintlock to percussion cap actions.[23]

At the head of the Confederate train, Scurry and the 310 men of Raguet's battalion of the Fourth Regiment hurried north to the escarpment. Hastening to join Pyron, they turned down one of the many arroyo cuts to the broad river bottom, with the slower artillery lagging behind. The battalion struck the flatland about two miles east of the river and hastened forward, taking a position on Pyron's right.

With the addition of Raguet's battalion, the Confederates now had about five hundred men at the ford, facing about the same number of Federals. They had also been bolstered by the arrival of one of Reily's twelve-pounder mountain howitzers, which took up a position on the far left. As Reily's second twelve-pounder started down the draw from the mesa top, the gunners heard the first deep explosions of the Union batteries opening fire from the east bank.

The Confederates were armed with a potpourri of weaponry, including smoothbore muskets, a few rifled muskets, shotguns, fowling pieces, and pistols.[24] In fact, some jested that the Second Texas Mounted Rifles (Baylor's command) should really be called the "Second Texas Mounted Shotguns." Knowing the shotgun's lethality and range limitations, a soldier so armed would want to close as quickly as possible (probably to within about fifty yards).

Indeed, as Private B. H. Tyler of Company F of the Fourth Regiment pointed out, buckshot presents a much deadlier pattern than a single-shot musket if one gets close enough to the enemy to use it:

> On leaving home we gathered up all the old shotguns and rifles we could. I had an old shotgun that had 2 barrels but only 1 lock, and it was a fair sample, but they did effective work as they sent 15 buckshot into them at a time.[25]

In addition to bringing the shotgun into effective range, the act of closing so aggressively would also have an effect on the troops being assaulted. This effect could be greatly amplified if the troops under attack were as inexperienced as the New Mexico Volunteers.

The Texans had deployed as dismounted cavalry, meaning that 375–400 of the men went forward.[26] They had just taken up a defensive position when they came under fire from the dismounted Federal troopers. Although the size and consistency of the opposing forces were comparable, the Texans' defensive position behind the sand embankment of the dry riverbed was a stronger one.

Scurry, however, was not satisfied with simply maintaining the defensive status quo. Perhaps sensing some tentativeness on the part of the Union leadership, he decided to attempt to control the lower ford from the downstream side and prevent the Federal artillery, which could be seen arriving on the west bank, from establishing a completely protected position from which to bombard the Confederates near the foot of the mesa. He dispatched a strong force of dismounted cavalry acting as skirmishers, together with one (or perhaps both) of Reily's recently arrived mountain howitzers,[27] to the heavy bosque at the edge of the mesa below the ford.

Lieutenant Colonel Roberts and his Federal infantry arrived at the ford slightly ahead of the artillery. With him rode First Lieutenant Charles Meinhold, a young officer who had been confined in irons at Fort Bliss for speaking out against the "secessionists." After escaping, he made his way across the Sierra Blanca to Fort Craig, where he was appointed to Canby's staff. He would serve with distinction on this February day.[28]

Noting the Texans' move to gain the foothold below the ford, Roberts immediately dispatched a messenger to Duncan, alerting him to the problem. In addition, he ordered Company K of the Fifth U.S. Infantry (Captain David Brotherton) to ford the river and deploy as skirmishers to reinforce the dismounted cavalry operating in the bosque.[29]

As soon as he received the word from Roberts, Duncan ordered Company C of the Third Cavalry under George Washington Howland, a captain from Rhode Island, to move to the right and support Irish-born Captain Edward Treacy, whose Company, D of the Third U.S. Cavalry, had been placed on the right as skirmishers when the cavalry had first crossed the river.

Several minutes of spirited fighting ensued, with control of the critical bosque seesawing back and forth. Finally, Duncan's men, now up to about 440 with the addition of Brotherton's infantry, gained a slight upper hand and the Texans retreated to the sandbank.[30]

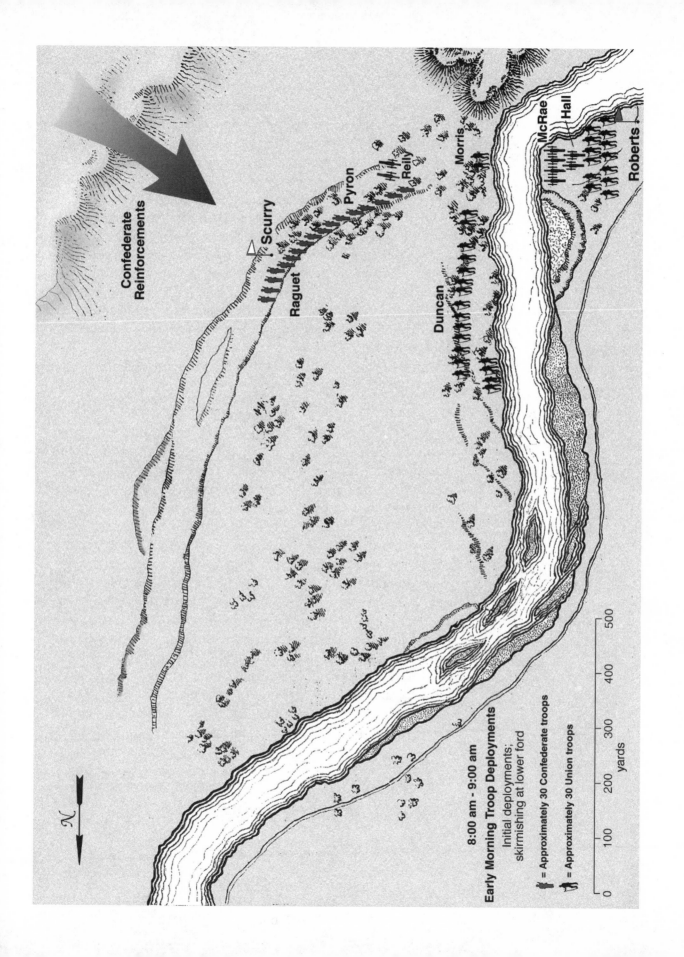

N

Confederate Reinforcements

Scurry

Raguet

Pyron

Reily

Morris

Duncan

McRae

Hall

Roberts

8:00 am - 9:00 am
Early Morning Troop Deployments
Initial deployments;
skirmishing at lower ford

= Approximately 30 Confederate troops

= Approximately 30 Union troops

0   100   200   300   400   500
yards

The Federal artillery arrived not long after Roberts and the infantry. Two of the sections—probably the twelve-pounders (three field howitzers and one mountain howitzer)—were part of the six-gun battery under the command of Alexander McRae, a West Pointer from North Carolina who had given his allegiance to country rather than to state.[31] This artillery company had been formed from companies of the Second and Third U.S. Cavalry in early November 1861. The sections themselves were headed up by Lieutenants Joseph McLellan Bell and Lyman Mishler. Twenty-four-year-old Lieutenant Robert Hall, a West Pointer from Illinois, commanded two twenty-four-pounder howitzers, the heaviest Federal artillery at Fort Craig.

Roberts placed the batteries on the west bank near the lower ford and directed their fire at the heavily wooded area being contested by Duncan on the opposite shore.

9:30-10:00 A.M., February 21, 1862, Confederate Train, Southeast of Mesa del Contadero

While Scurry dispatched four companies to Valverde to reinforce Pyron, the rest of the Fourth had formed in column and struck off from the train "at a brisk trot." Just as Private Frank Starr and the rest of Reily's artillery detachment reached the bottom of the draw, the remainder of Scurry's force came thundering by.[32]

Despite their thirst and the certainty of the impending fight, the troopers were apparently in high spirits and, "singing songs," rode quickly across the valley to a location on Raguet's right, behind the embankment. There, they secured their horses and took cover, listening to the almost constant bursts of small-arms fire. Fortunately, at least for the time being, the Federal fire was principally devoted to the men of Pyron's and Raguet's commands farther down the embankment.

The men of the Fourth Regiment did not have much respite. Soon, they too became the target of Duncan's troopers and elected to "lie low" and wait for what they hoped would be the imminent arrival of more Confederate artillery.

Across the river on the Union side, Lieutenant Colonel Roberts was growing increasingly frustrated. From his vantage point, he could see

Confederate reinforcements, including more artillery, arriving in the bosque along the north face of the mesa. He was also acutely aware of the strategic importance of the wooded areas on the east bank, across from the lower ford, having reconnoitered the area some weeks before in anticipation of just such an engagement.[33] He had hoped to move his artillery to the east bank almost immediately, and he had counted on Duncan to clear the bosque to permit this crossing. The east bank position would have allowed him to target the relatively exposed Texans more effectively as they struggled down the arroyo to reinforce the Confederate position.

Three times Roberts sent messengers, including his adjutant, Lieutenant Meinhold, splashing across the cold water to implore Duncan to move more aggressively. Although he later estimated that Duncan would only have had to hold the area for about twenty minutes for the batteries to cross, the cavalry commander seemed unable (or unwilling) to drive the Confederates out of their bastion behind the first sand embankment, which dominated the bosque.[34]

Finally, Roberts dispatched another aide, Lieutenant W. W. Mills, with a message to Canby that the enemy's main force would reach the ford before noon and that reinforcements were needed.[35]

Thus, while the Federal artillery remained on the west bank, the Texans continued to strengthen their position relatively unimpeded.

10:00 A.M., February 21, 1862, With the Confederate Train

Teel, informed of the departure of a large enemy force (probably Roberts and half of the garrison) from Fort Craig,[36] ordered Lieutenants Joseph McGuinness and Jordan Bennett to take charge of the two guns near the rear of the train and then moved to the front of the column, where Lieutenant Bradford had the remaining two-gun section of the artillery company. As he neared the front of the column, he heard the distant sounds of the firefight, including the first deep booms of cannons, echoing from Valverde. Taking personal charge of the six-pounders, Teel galloped off to the ford with Bradford. According to Teel, the cannons were at the battlefield and "placed in battery within a few minutes".[37]

At Fort Craig, Colonel Canby anxiously awaited news from the battlefield. Since the ford was not visible from the fort, he relied on informa-

Captain Henry Selden, Fifth U.S. Infantry. Courtesy Special Collections Division, U.S. Military Academy Library.

tion from scouts assigned primarily to Graydon and stationed atop the mesa, as well as couriers from his field commanders at the various locations.[38]

With Green's 840 men deployed between the campsite and the southern edge of the mesa and Sibley's intentions still unclear, Canby had kept a sizable force on the eastern shore across from Fort Craig.[39] However, when Lieutenant Mills arrived with the message from Roberts, it finally became clear that Sibley intended to seize the ford and not the fort. Therefore, the Union commander elected to commit most of the remainder of his forces to support the developing battle at Valverde.

First, Captain Henry Selden's battalion of 640 men, eight companies of regular infantry[40] plus Dodd's Colorado Volunteers, were ordered to cross the river downstream from the fort and report to Roberts at the lower ford. Shortly thereafter, Carson and the 460 men in his seven companies of New Mexico Volunteers were issued similar orders.[41] This left 590 men of the Second New Mexico Volunteers plus the 300 militiamen under Major Wesche and Colonel Pino on the eastern bank south of the mesa as an advanced guard against any attempts to attack Fort Craig from the south or the east.

10:45 A.M., February 21, 1862, Confederate Right Wing above the Lower Ford

Shortly after Raguet's reinforcements arrived, Teel and Bradford galloped up and unlimbered two six-pounders immediately in front of the Fourth Texas Regiment's position.[42] Immediately, they opened a brisk fire and a spirited artillery duel commenced.

The longer-range Federal artillery took its toll on the Confederate gunners, and Teel soon found himself with only five gunners for his two pieces and one dead and three wounded men lying behind the sand-bank. Requesting reinforcements from Scurry, Teel continued to fight, alternating fire between the two pieces and, at times, ramming home shells himself.[43]

Reily's twelve-pounders had been driven from the lower bosque by the early fire of the longer-range Federal batteries on the western shore. One of the two guns continued to fire sporadically on the Union skirmishers in the bosque, but the other had been withdrawn by Lieutenant Colonel Scurry. With Teel running short of gunners in the center of the Texas line, Scurry dispatched some men from Reily's disengaged battery up the line to replace Teel's losses.

Sometime before noon the situation became even "hotter" as exploding Union shells periodically set the dry grama grass on fire around Teel's six-pounders.[44] After a short time, the Federal artillery changed its front. Now their target was Pyron. This gave the battered Texans of Teel's battery a brief chance to regroup. Teel ordered his six-pounders limbered and they moved off to the left down the Confederate line.

6

Apparent Victory

Late Morning, February 21, 1862, Union Position
on the East Bank, Lower Ford

MAJOR DUNCAN AND THE ELEVEN COMPANIES IN HIS UNION BATTALION
were spread over several hundred yards of east-bank bosque about 180
yards east of the river.[1] Lieutenant Ira Claflin (later to be breveted for
gallantry at Gettysburg), who had first detected the movement of the
Texas cavalry near the upper ford, remained on the left and Captain
Robert Morris, a twice-breveted Mexican War veteran, was in overall
command of the men who were deployed as skirmishers on the far right.

Unsure of the Confederate's true strength and unable to discern it
because of the thick underbrush and sand hills, Duncan was reluctant to
pursue the Texans aggressively. Moreover, Rebel artillery had been regu-
larly raking the Union position. Instead of advancing, Duncan merely
consolidated his position and sent some of the skirmishers to harass the
Texans as they attempted to reconnoiter the Federal position.

Although the battle for the east-bank bosque at the lower ford had
continued since before 8:00 A.M., casualties appear to have been rather
light.[2] The Confederates (Pyron and Raguet, with Scurry to their right)
had kept up a constant fire of small arms and six- and twelve-pounders,
effectively keeping Duncan from moving out from between the heavy
woods and the river. On the other hand, the heavy shelling from McRae
and Hall on the west bank, plus fire from the men of Howland's, Treacy's,
and Brotherton's commands, effectively blunted the Confederates' advance and stymied efforts to anchor their left on the riverbank below the
lower ford.

Finally, a well-placed shell, perhaps from one of Hall's twenty-four-
pounders, put one of the two six-pounders (under Bradford) out of com-

mission. The men of the section were forced to withdraw, leaving the cannon, together with its damaged limbers and dead horses, in place. Without this forward artillery support, the Texans were unable to keep Duncan from moving into the bosque, and the Union right was finally able to consolidate its position at the lower ford.

As noon approached, confident that Duncan's position was now secure (albeit much later and closer to the river than he had hoped), Roberts turned his full attention to the Confederate right. He moved McRae's cannons to the middle ford and ordered Selden, recently arrived from south of the mesa with Wingate's and Plympton's infantry battalions, to cross at the middle ford, about one-half mile north, and to form to Duncan's left.[3] Selden's orders were to fix bayonets and drive the Texans from the bosque north of Duncan's position. If only Duncan would advance on the right, with Selden advancing on the left, Roberts was "undoubting in [his] conviction...that the rout would have been complete".[4]

Roberts was also concerned by a report that a sizable body of Confederate cavalry, perhaps as large as five hundred men, might have crossed the river a mile or two north of the battlefield near the village of Valverde, intending to threaten the Union rear. He therefore dispatched Carson and his mounted volunteers, who had ridden to the ford just behind Selden, to move north along the west bank on the main road and take a defensive position in the west-bank bosque, north of the middle ford.[5]

Late Morning, February 21, 1862, Confederate Train
East of Mesa del Contadero

Sibley, increasingly concerned over the Federal success on his left, sent a courier to Green ordering him to proceed to Valverde "with all his disposable force" to reinforce Scurry and Pyron.[6] Green directed Lieutenant Colonel Sutton with his Seventh Regiment, supplemented by Companies C and H of the Fifth, to remain with the northbound wagons.[7] Then he and Major Lockridge took the remaining eight companies of the Fifth, about 670 men, plus one section of the regimental artillery (two twelve-pounder mountain howitzers under Lieutenant William Wood) and proceeded to the battlefield "with as much speed as practicable."[8]

Green and Lockridge arrived between 12:30 and 1:00, just as Selden's battalion was splashing across the river. Green positioned five of his companies in the gap that had opened between Pyron and Raguet and sent three companies of the Fifth (probably D, K, and H), under twenty-four-year-old Lieutenant Colonel Henry C. McNeill, to the far left to reinforce Pyron. Lieutenant Wood and the twelve-pounders stayed on the right, while Pyron and his troops moved up the old riverbed to a position at the left center.

Three Confederate battalions were now deployed at the ford. On the left was one battalion of three companies of the Fifth (McNeill) and four companies of the Fourth (Raguet), for a total of 520 men, and one of Teel's guns; in the center, Green and Lockridge directed five companies of the Fifth, Pyron's battalion, plus one of Teel's howitzers and one of Reily's twelve-pounder mountain howitzers (630 men and two guns); on the right, Lieutenant Colonel Scurry had the rest of the Fourth plus Wood's two mountain howitzers and one of Teel's six-pounders (630 men and three guns).[9] Bradford's abandoned six-pounder with its dead horses and Reily's damaged mountain howitzer lay forward of the Confederate left.

Lockridge, McNeill, and Raguet, realizing that their goal of pushing the Federals from the lower bosque had gone awry, were unwilling to further compound the deteriorating position by losing Bradford's abandoned, but still apparently functional, cannon. Captains A. J. Scarborough and William Alexander were ordered to move forward and retrieve the gun. The task facing the young officers and their men was not an easy one. Not only were they exposed to galling artillery fire, but they had to retrieve a cannon whose team lay dead in harness. Moving forward under intense fire, the volunteers raced to the cannon and cut the traces. Then, dragging and pushing the heavy weapon, they manhandled it back to the safety of the Confederate lines. Raguet felt fortunate to have only one of the men killed and "a few" wounded—a small price to pay for a precious piece of artillery.[10]

Bradford's gun was set up with Reily's remaining mountain howitzer, and it resumed service defending the Confederate left. However, because he was short of gunners and out of longer-range round shot, Raguet had the rescued cannon double-shotted with canister and left in position in anticipation of a Federal charge. He then withdrew further up the riverbed with one of Lieutenant Wood's twelve-pounder mountain howitzers, which had been moved down from the right.[11]

Sometime after noon Lieutenant Colonel Sutton, the expatriate New

Yorker now in command of the Confederate supply train, received a message from Green: The situation at the ford was deteriorating and Sutton was directed to reinforce as quickly as possible, even at the risk of leaving the train with a substantially reduced escort. Sutton promptly ordered Companies A and H of the Seventh and Captain Denman Shannon's C of the Fifth to remain with the train with four of the twelve-pounder light howitzers—two each from the Fourth and Fifth regiments.[12] He then proceeded to the ford "at a gallop" with Companies B, F, and I of the Seventh under battalion command of Captain Powhatan Jordan, a medical doctor from Virginia who had settled in San Antonio, and Company F of the Fifth under Tennessean George Washington Campbell.

Met by Lockridge, Sutton's men were directed to the left center, where they were almost immediately brought under heavy fire, losing two men and three horses in about an hour.[13]

Late Morning, February 21, 1862, Union Position near the Southwestern Edge of Mesa del Contadero

Sometime before noon, pickets from Wesche's battalion of New Mexico Militia spotted three companies of mounted Confederates (about 250 men) moving along the trail below the southeastern edge of the mesa.[14] Quickly, the major ordered his outnumbered troops into line of battle, and the 108 men moved around the southern tip of the mesa toward the oncoming Confederates.

Preparing to engage at a distance of about eighty yards, the inexperienced Union volunteers must have felt much relieved to find their numbers suddenly trebled by the arrival of Colonel Nicholas Pino and Lieutenant Colonel Jesús M. Baca y Salazar, together with the two hundred additional mounted New Mexico militiamen who had been on patrol on the east bank south of the mesa for the past two days.

The Confederates, realizing that their numerical advantage had disappeared, turned around and moved back toward the northeast after exchanging a few desultory shots.

Anxious to exploit his momentary advantage, Wesche ordered Captains Sena y Rivera and Sanchez to pursue the retreating Texans. However, before the two companies could recover their horses and leave, Canby's adjutant, J. C. Clever, arrived with the news that several abandoned Confederate wagons had been sighted south of the mesa near the previous night's campsite. Wesche was ordered to proceed to that location and ensure that the wagons were cut off from the army at the ford. The major immediately countermanded his order to pursue, and the small force moved off to the southeast toward the Confederate campsite.

Noon, February 21, 1862, Fort Craig

Throughout the morning, Colonel Canby anxiously received reports from his forces both north of and atop the mesa. As a dust cloud announced the movement of Green and the men of the Fifth Texas north from the campsite, Canby was convinced. This was no feint, but rather a full-blown attempt on Sibley's part to secure the ford. Thus, once he was told that Wesche and the New Mexico Militia had turned back the Texans south of the mesa, Canby felt that he must commit himself to the ford.

The colonel immediately recalled Miguel Pino and the Second New Mexico Mounted Volunteers from the east bank. He then headed for the ford himself, accompanied by the two remaining six-pounders of McRae's battery and Captain Richard S. C. Lord's company of Regulars (D of the First Cavalry).[15] Before leaving, Canby delegated command of the fort to Colonel Manuel Armijo of the First New Mexico Militia and Colonel Gabriel René Paul, a West Pointer and breveted veteran of the Mexican and Seminole wars.[16] They commanded a detachment of about one thousand men—two companies of volunteers, the New Mexico Militia, and "some detachments of regular troops."[17]

12:30 P.M., February 21, 1862, Middle Ford, West Bank[18]

Captain Selden of the Fifth U.S. Infantry put Captain Benjamin Wingate in charge of his right and Captain Peter Plympton, an 1843 West Point graduate, in command of his left. Together they led the regulars from the Fifth, Seventh, and Tenth infantries, plus Dodd's company of Colorado Volunteers, across the icy, armpit-deep water. On the east bank the battalion was joined on the right by Chacón's company, detached from Duncan's left, resulting in a combined force of about 630 infantry and dismounted cavalry.

Colonel Gabriel René Paul, Fourth NM Volunteers, shown after promotion to brigadier general. Courtesy The Library of Congress.

Captain Benjamin Wingate, Fifth U.S. Infantry. Courtesy Museum of New Mexico, neg. no. 13115.

Sheltered from the intermittent snow flurries by the trees about six hundred yards from the Rebel lines, the infantry fixed bayonets and the troopers drew their sabres. After the distinctive (and, no doubt, unnerving) clicking of the knives and swords subsided, the force aligned itself. With a quick check up and down the line, the order was given and the battalion moved forward through the woods.

The Texans under Lieutenant Colonel Scurry had had a relatively easy time of it thus far—Pyron's and Raguet's men had taken most of the Federal artillery and small-arms fire during the morning on the Confederate left. Scurry had deployed skirmishers along the edge of the woods a few hundred yards in front of the first sand ridge near the old riverbank;

but fearing he was badly outnumbered, he had not attempted to challenge the Federals in his front. Now the men of the Fourth Texas raised their heads and noticed Selden's Federal infantry crossing the river and deploying in a line of attack in the thick bosque. Concerned that this move could flank his position, Scurry ordered the battalion, together with Reily's mountain howitzers, back to their horses. They quickly moved about 250 yards to their right, extending the Texas line up the dry riverbed.[19]

The Fourth Regiment was totally unprepared for the intensity of the initial Federal assault. As they dismounted and moved to the embankment, higher here than in their earlier location, the men of the Fourth Texas Volunteers came under a hail of small-arms fire that took a heavy toll on the horses, as well as wounding some of the men. Private Al Field was shot through the arm, S. Schmidt was shot through both thighs, and William Onderdonk was shot in the mouth and cut out part of his tongue with his own knife before being carried to the rear.[20] Despite these setbacks, the Texans maintained their composure and continued to fight back.

As Selden's men got within a few hundred yards of the embankment, their rifle fire wreaked greater and greater havoc. Later, Captain Rafael Chacón would write that the charge was so violent

> that in a quarter of an hour that renown enemy cavalry was left stretched out on the ground, completely destroyed, their horses and men dead and dying on the field.[21]

Like Lieutenant Meinhold, William Mills, another officer on Canby's staff, had also been held in chains by Baylor and the Texans.[22] He described the charge from another Union perspective:

> the 5th, now the 'bloody 5th,' advanced steadily and for a few moments evry thing [sic] was quiet, the stillness which proceeds [sic] the storm. Presently came a voley [sic] from the 5th then a return from the Texans followed by continual sputtering of marketry [sic], drowned occasionally by the cheers of our brave men as 'the men borne [sic] insensible to fear' gave way from clump after clump of cottonwoods and retreated toward the hills. When Captain Selden was ordered to advance with less than 600 men it was not supposed that the enemies

main body had yet arrived at the bosque but he soon found that he had charged into the center of probably 2,000 men and being flanked on both sides, he retired in good order to the river bank.[23]

By 2:30 P.M., the line of Union skirmishers had closed within effective range of the Texans. Sergeant Peticolas recalled:

> myself and a number of others who had minie guns fired upon them with sufficient rapidity to very well reply to their fire...they began to pay dearly for getting so close to us. Not a man shot without taking sight, for Texas boys are accustomed to the use of arms and never shoot away their ammunition for nothing. Although our balls were not as numerous as theirs, they went with more deadly intent, and our fire soon became extremely galling.[24]

Despite these localized successes, Scurry found himself spread dangerously thin. Only two companies, Hardeman's and Crosson's, occupied his far right and a gap had opened between that contingent and the other four companies of the Fourth Regiment. Even though he held a position of strength behind the embankment and he had slowed the Federal advance, Scurry was increasingly concerned that he was dangerously outnumbered.

The fact that they were outnumbered didn't seem to bother the men of the Fourth. Certainly they were thirsty; but demoralized—absolutely not! Peticolas relates that one of the men spotted a wounded Federal soldier lying in front of the lines. Approaching Captain Nunn (Company I of the Fourth Mounted Volunteers), he asked,

> Captain, yonder is a damned son-of-a-bitch that I have shot who is lying behind a tree shooting at us. May I go out and kill him? Captain Nunn gave permission and he went out but the man begged so hard that he did not kill him but got four minie guns and ammunition and brought them back to the bank.[25]

Even though Selden's advance had been slowed, Roberts felt confident that both his left and right were secure and he was determined to cross his artillery and intensify the pressure on the Texans. The six cannons, both of Hall's twenty-four-pounders and McRae's four twelve-pounders, were quickly limbered up and moved to the middle ford, where they splashed across at a gallop to a position on Selden's right. In sup-

Captain James "Santiago" Hubbell, Fifth NM Volunteers. New Mexico State Records Center and Archives, Hubbell Collection, no. 12306.

port of the battery, Roberts placed Brotherton and Ingraham's regulars and Hubbell and Mortimore's volunteers.

Connecticut-born James Lawrence Hubbell had enlisted in the army in 1846 at the age of twenty. Sent to garrison duty in New Mexico, Hubbell was mustered out in Santa Fe in 1847 and quickly married a local heiress, Juliana Gutierrez, whose father had bequeathed her forty-five thousand acres on the Pajarito land grant. Assimilating into the local population and becoming a prosperous trader, Hubbell soon came to be known as Santiago. He reenlisted in November 1861 and was assigned as the captain of Company B of the Fifth New Mexico Volunteers.[26]

As quickly as they had been limbered, McRae's artillery unlimbered and resumed firing. The Federals immediately opened against the Confederate cannons with sustained counter-battery fire. Meanwhile, Hall moved his twenty-four-pounders to the extreme right. Here, he attempted to dislodge a large party of skirmishers that had been reported by Captain Morris to have infiltrated back into the bosque adjacent to the mesa.

As this was happening, Rafael Chacón and his company of New Mexico Volunteers, having moved back to the right after Selden's advance had stalled, noted an unmanned cannon to their front in the bosque (this was apparently the twelve-pounder that Scarborough and the men of the Fourth Texas had retrieved, double-shotted, then abandoned). Moving forward with his company, Chacón had Corporal Leyba (a cousin of his wife, Juanita) "lasso" the piece and drag it, "cowboy style," back to the Federal lines.

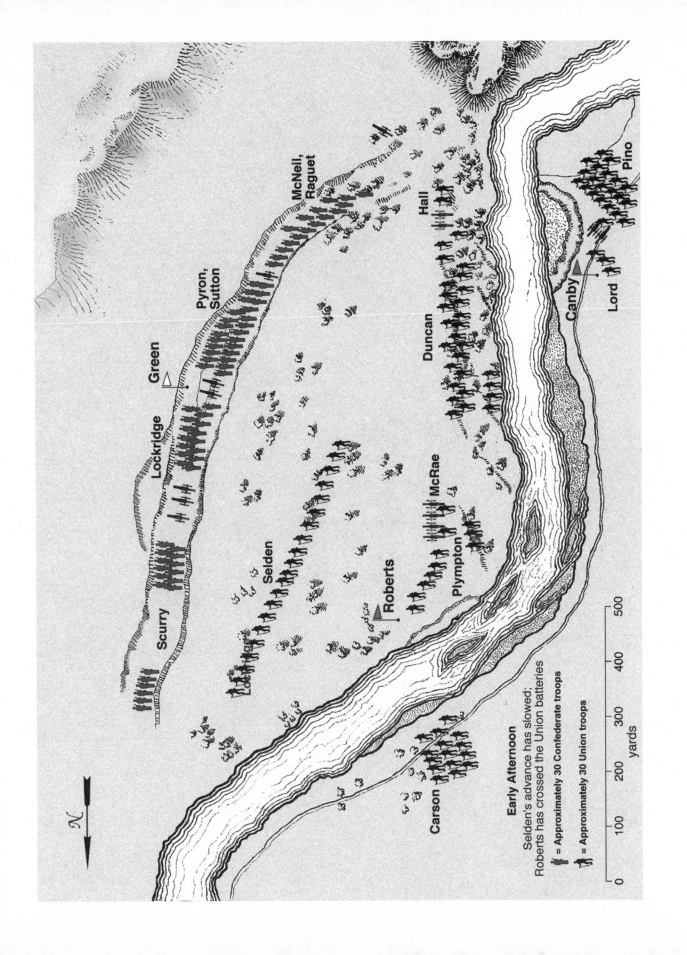

Scurry

Lockridge

Green

Pyron,
Sutton

McNeil,
Raguet

Selden

Lockridge

Roberts

Hall

Duncan

McRae

Plympton

Carson

Canby

Lord

Pino

N

Early Afternoon

Selden's advance has slowed;
Roberts has crossed the Union batteries

= Approximately 30 Confederate troops

= Approximately 30 Union troops

0   100   200   300   400   500

yards

A. B. Peticolas's pencil sketch of operations on the Confederate left flank. The two cannons facing the Confederate left are Hall's twenty-four-pounders. From Alberts, *Rebels on the Rio Grande* (1984) and used with the permission of the family.

7

Change of Command

**2:00–2:30 P.M., February 21, 1862,
Northern Edge of the Battlefield[1]**

ALTHOUGH THE UNION ADVANCE AT THE CENTER AND RIGHT HAD slowed, the Union left continued to move steadily toward Scurry's thinned ranks on the extreme Confederate right. Peering through the battlefield haze toward this Federal advance, the Confederates now thought they saw uniforms that were clearly not Union regulars. Thinking this part of the Federal force to be easily intimidated New Mexico Volunteers, Colonel Green ordered two cavalry companies to charge the extreme right of Canby's line. Such a move would disrupt the Union advance and prevent these troops from turning the Confederate's right flank.

The cavalry units chosen by Green for the maneuver were two of the fabled lancer companies that several Confederate brigades had mustered into service in the grand tradition of the Napoleonic cavalier. An anachronism by the outbreak of the Civil War—though one still favored by many senior officers on both sides—the troopers were armed with nine-foot lances, each tipped with twelve-inch blades and sporting red guidon banners, emblazoned with a single white star.[2] In parade and formation, these riders provided a glimpse of the glory days of the eighteenth century, but in this battle they would prove to be no match for rifled muskets and minié balls.

Although none of the cavalrymen had ever ridden into battle with their "hog pokers," Jerome McCown, one of their captains, and other Confederate officers had been favorably impressed by the "dash and glitter" of the lancers he had seen during the Mexican War.[3] McCown was also famous for a prayer he allegedly had offered before going into battle in Mexico and which he may well have repeated at Valverde:

Oh, Lord, we are about to join battle with a vastly superior number of the enemy, and, Heavenly Father, we would mightily like for you to be on our side and help us; but if you can't do it, for Christ's sake don't go over to the Mexicans but lie low and keep dark and you'll see one of the damndest fights you ever saw in all your born days! Amen.[4]

A call of the bugle and Captain Willis Lang and about seventy lancers trotted out from behind the sand embankment. The column turned smartly and headed northwest toward the waiting Federals, about three hundred yards away. (Unfortunately for Lang and his men, the order to charge may actually have been countermanded by Green at the last minute, but this change was heard only by Captain McCown and his men and not by Lang.)[5]

Much to the later chagrin of the lancers, the men in different uniforms seen by Green and the Texans were not inexperienced New Mexicans, but the seventy-one members of the Colorado Volunteers, commanded by Captain Theodore Dodd.[6] Anticipating the threat as he watched the Texas lancers move out from behind the embankment and form for their charge, Dodd assembled his company into the classic hollow square, one of the period's defensive tactics against cavalry.[7] As the troopers closed on the square, Dodd's men could see the lance blades gleaming and the red guidons streaming.

At a range of between fifty and one hundred yards, Dodd raised his sword and shouted, "They're Texans! Give'em Hell!" and the Coloradans opened fire with a combination of buckshot and round shot known as "buck and ball."[8] In a hail of lead, horses and riders tumbled to the ground in a bloody mass. The few riders fortunate enough to survive the first volley cleared the cloud of dust and smoke only to face another fearsome volley and the fixed bayonets of the Union infantry.

Ickis described the charge:

the boys waited until they got within 40 yards of us when they took deliberate aim and it was fun to see the Texans fall. They wavered for a few moments then on they came and fierce looking fellows they were with their long lances raised but when they got to us we were loaded again and then we gave them the "buck and ball." After the second volley there were but a few of them left and but one of them got away.

Captain Theodore Dodd, Colorado Volunteers, shown after promotion to colonel. Courtesy Colorado Historical Society.

The others were shot [and] one bayoneted. G. Simpson ran his bayonet through one of them and shot the top of his head off.[9]

Almost as soon as it had started the charge was over, and the bloodied remnants of Lang's glorious parade-ground troopers crawled and staggered back to the protection of the embankment. Behind them lay twenty dead and wounded lancers.[10] In addition, virtually all of the horses that had started the charge were killed or maimed. Captain Lang himself was "grievously wounded." Lingering in agony for nine days, he requested a pistol from a slave and finished the job that Dodd and his men had started.[11]

Lang's second-in-command, Lieutenant Demetrius Bass, was also wounded in the abortive charge. His arm was so badly shattered that it had to be amputated. Despite the radical surgery, he too died a few days later.

Those men who did manage to return unscathed (and, no doubt, the other lancers who had watched in horror from behind the embankment) wisely threw down their lances and rearmed themselves with pistols and rifles and continued the fight on a more even basis. In addition, after the battle they apparently placed the useless "hog pokers" in a pile and burned them. Ickis remarked that they must have realized that "they were not the things to fight Colorado Volunteers with."[12] (Remarkably, Dodd's company apparently repulsed the charge without a single casualty.)[13] According to Steuart, this was the only organized use of lances or pikes in combat in the Civil War, even though several units were armed with the archaic weapons.[14]

Futile as it was, the charge was viewed by some as one of the most heroic of the war. Green later described it as "one of the most gallant and furious charges ever witnessed in the annals of battle," and Scurry characterized it as showing "desperate courage." It did have an important tactical effect. Lang's charge "desynchronized" Selden's advance sufficiently that it stalled and the forward elements moved back to the river.[15] Near the center of the Confederate line, Peticolas noticed: "After the fight had been kept up for about half an hour, they retreated precipitously toward the river."[16]

In addition, the distraction allowed Teel to move two six-pounders from the center of the Confederate line to the extreme right. Bringing the fire of these cannons to bear on the Federal left, along with the muskets and shotguns of Hardeman's and Crosson's companies, Scurry was able to stem the Union advance and force the rest of the Union infantry to withdraw. At least for a time, this prevented his right from being turned.

Soon after the lancers' abortive charge, the intensity of the battle abated. Roberts's opportunity to mass his force to roll up the Confederate left had evaporated with the arrival of Green's troops and the establishment of a strengthened defensive position in the old riverbed.

alry, Brotherton's infantry company, and one of the two twenty-four-pounders of Hall's battery.[19] This group had temporarily halted below the bend in the old riverbed while the men rested and rearmed. Across the river, Carson, Miguel Pino, and Lord formed a Union reserve force of about 1,250 men.

When he arrived on the field, Colonel Canby immediately sought out Roberts. After a quick but formal assumption of command and a personal reconnaissance of the Federal position, the Federal leaders conferred and a strategy emerged to break the apparent impasse. Canby worried that a "direct attack upon [the Confederate] position would be attended with great loss and would be of doubtful result."[20] Therefore, he decided to move McRae's battery about two hundred yards north and slightly forward to a position where it could be "anchored" to the riverbank by supporting infantry and where it could bring the Confederate right, including the pesky battery which had materialized in the wake of the lancer attack, under concentrated fire.[21] Canby then planned to adopt Roberts's strategy and advance his right, supported by Hall's remaining twenty-four-pounder, like a huge door, slamming up the Texans' left. To prevent a breakout, Carson and Wingate would anchor the center. With the plan agreed upon, Canby dispatched Roberts to the center of the line south of the battery, and he assumed personal control of the left.

After ordering the six cannons and eighty-five men of McRae's battery to move, Canby positioned Plympton's battalion behind the riverbank. He deployed Company A of the Tenth Infantry (under command of Captain George Rossell) as skirmishers on the far left and Company F of the Seventh Infantry (under Sergeant James Rockwell) in line of battle on the far right. Between these units were Companies H of the Tenth Infantry, C and H of the Seventh, and Dodd's Coloradans. The two companies of New Mexico Volunteers were positioned slightly closer to the battery and forward of the Tenth Infantry—Mortimore's company on the left with Hubbell to his immediate right.[22]

Thus, the Federal left had McRae's battery directly supported by Hubbell's and Mortimore's companies of New Mexico Volunteers and backed up by regulars and Colorado Volunteers from Plympton's battalion, for a total of about 630 men. In the center, able to move to support either Canby or Roberts, were 770 men from Wingate's battalion and Carson's regiment. The reserve consisted of Pino's 590 New Mexico Volunteers (still arriving on the west bank) and the First U.S. Cavalry (Captains Lord and Claflin under battalion command of Lord, currently near the river on the eastern shore) for a reserve force that now totaled about 720.

On the right, Duncan commanded about 630 men—the dismounted regular cavalry, Valdez's volunteer cavalry, and Brotherton's infantry company. The remaining Federal troops and militia were either at Fort Craig or with Colonel Nicholas Pino and Major Wesche south of the mesa.[23]

Behind the sand hills, out of sight of the Federal troops, the Confederates were also realigning. Sibley, suffering from a "colic" that he treated with heavy doses of whiskey, had not been a factor in the battle so far, even though he was in titular command of the Texas forces. About 1:30 P.M., he acknowledged his incapacity and sent his staff to report to Colonel Green, near the Confederate center, while he retired to his ambulance in the Confederate rear.[24]

As late as 3:00 P.M., the Texans were still thinking about defense. In order to stop the Union advance, Scurry, in command of about 470 men of the Fourth, had been forced to extend his line farther to the right. Green had placed most of the Fifth Regiment, about 790 men, in the center with Lockridge and Sutton. Pyron, too, had moved the 180 men of his command to the left center of the Confederate line. On the left, Raguet had about 540 men, including McNeill's men of the Fifth. In addition, there were teamsters, wagonmasters, and bandsmen, plus 250 troopers under Denman Shannon, guarding the train east of the battlefield.[25]

As the sporadic firing continued and the afternoon shadows lengthened, the weary men on both sides wondered what each would do next.

8

The Tide Turns

3:00 P.M., February 21, 1862, Behind Confederate Lines

MAJOR SAMUEL LOCKRIDGE RECOGNIZED THAT HE FACED EVER-worsening odds. Both he and Raguet had asked Green for reinforcements, but the intensity of the action on the north end of the battlefield not only prevented Green from diverting troops to reinforce Raguet but necessitated the relocation of two of Teel's six-pounders (under Bennett and McGuiness) to the Confederate right. This meant that the beleaguered left had only a single twelve-pounder under the command of Lieutenant Reily.[1]

After a brief consultation, the Texans decided to leave the dry riverbed and move their forces one hundred yards to the rear to the shelter of another sandbank. After covering the movement of wounded and artillery, Raguet and Lockridge ordered the battalion to fall back by companies, and the relocation was accomplished in an orderly fashion.

The twenty-three hundred or so Confederates were now stretched over nearly a mile from McNeill and Raguet on the extreme left to Hardeman and Crosson on the far right. Within the ranks strode Lockridge and Scurry, encouraging the men to maintain the integrity of their line. A few yards behind the line, still protected by the embankment, rode Tom Green and his flamboyant aide-de-camp, Alabama-born Lieutenant Thomas Peck Ochiltree.[2]

3:30 P.M., February 21, 1862, Canby's Headquarters near McRae's Battery, Two Hundred Yards East of the Middle Ford

After McRae had positioned his four twelve-pounders on the southern end of the line with a slight separation from the two six-pounders to the north, Canby ordered him to bring the Confederate right under fire.[3] To support McRae's artillery, Captains Lord and Claflin were ordered to unite their companies and provide a cavalry reserve for the advanced battery. Aware that he had sent the battery into harm's way, Canby also sent orders to Pino's Second Regiment of New Mexico Volunteers—presently waiting on the west bank near the middle ford—to cross the river and join in supporting McRae.

Soon a lively firefight began, with McRae engaging the Confederate battery (under Teel) in an artillery duel. Plympton and his men hunkered down beneath the riverbank behind the battery, in a desperate effort to avoid the "very severe and concentrated fire of grape and rifle shot."[4]

As the artillery duel began, Lockridge rode to Green's headquarters on the Confederate right to ascertain his commander's intent. Learning that a decision to strengthen the right had been made, he rode back down the line and told Raguet to bring his men up to act as a cavalry reserve. Raguet's four companies quickly moved about six hundred yards north, staying behind the embankment to avoid attracting the unwelcome attention of the Federal artillery.

While Raguet was moving to the right, Colonel Green took stock of the evolving situation. Realizing that he had to slow the Federal advance on his left if he was to avoid the perilous position of having simultaneous Federal assaults on both of his flanks, Green countermanded his original order. Raguet was now ordered back to the left to "menace the enemy, now flanking us in large numbers."[5]

Raguet instantly countermarched his troopers. Trotting down the dry riverbed, they were back where they had started within a few minutes. Raguet quickly organized his forces to "menace the enemy." Joined by Captain Scarborough's company (B of the Fourth), he aligned about 250 men, and charged the Federal cannon (Hall's twenty-four-pounder), now drawn up and firing from a location several hundred yards to the southwest.[6] Because the Union troops were pivoting to the northeast and swinging up the old riverbank somewhat like a closing door, Raguet's charge took his battalion of infantry and cavalry on a diagonal course in front of the advancing Union forces.

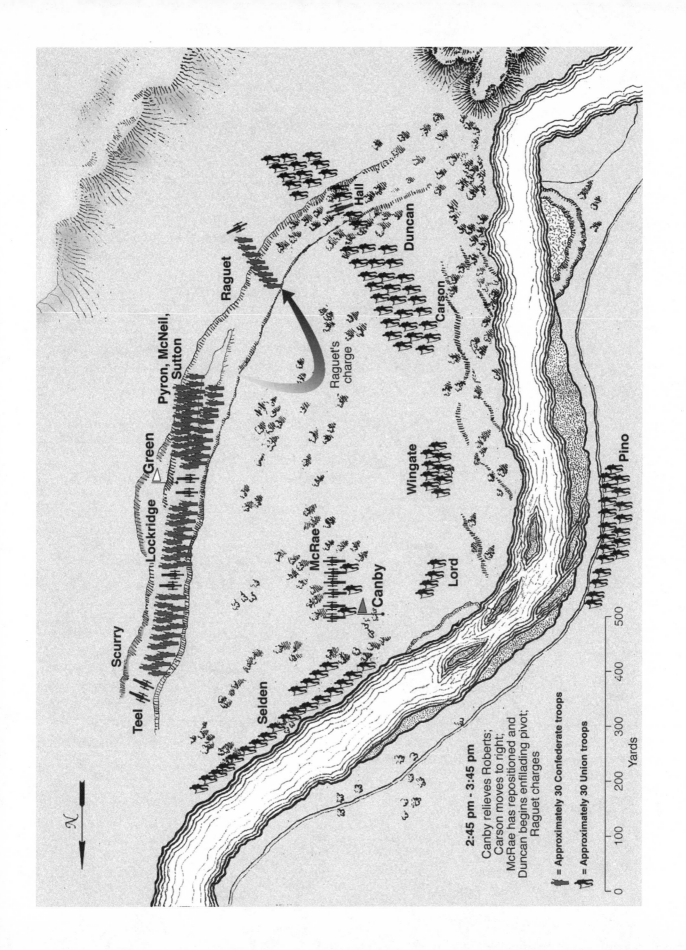

N

2:45 pm - 3:45 pm

Canby relieves Roberts;
Carson moves to right;
McRae has repositioned and
Duncan begins enfilading pivot;
Raguet charges

🏇 = Approximately 30 Confederate troops

🐎 = Approximately 30 Union troops

Teel

Scurry

Lockridge

Green

Pyron, McNeil, Sutton

Raguet

Raguet's charge

Selden

McRae

Canby

Lord

Wingate

Hall

Duncan

Carson

Pino

0   100   200   300   400   500

Yards

Duncan had been joined by Carson's First New Mexico Volunteers and Graydon's spy company sometime after 3:00 P.M., bringing this contingent of the Federal force to nearly twelve hundred men. Carson had been placed on Duncan's left, with Hall's twenty-four-pounder on the extreme right, protected by Valdez's New Mexico Volunteers.[7] From here they were able to press the Confederate left, coming closer and closer to being able to both enfilade the Confederate line and threaten their train.[8]

Ever since the morning's battle, fearing that he was outnumbered and might be counterattacked and perhaps even lose the lower ford with devastating results, Duncan had proceeded cautiously. When the Confederate cavalry (under Raguet) appeared on his left, moving toward his single remaining twenty-four-pounder, Duncan dispatched a courier to Canby, urgently requesting reinforcements. In the meantime, he suspended his wheeling maneuver, opting instead to defend his current position against the advancing Texans.

As the charging Confederates came within one to two hundred yards, the Federals opened fire. The devastating volley rocked Raguet. At nearly the same time, a well-placed round from the twenty-four-pounder exploded in the middle of the Texan lines. Sergeant M. D. Oliver of Company F of the Fourth Texas Mounted Volunteers recalled:

> They repulsed us within 75 yards of their line. At this point it appeared that minie balls and grapeshot were as thick as hail but God preserved our lives and we lost but few men but our horses suffered badly.[9]

Raguet, at the head of the charge, glanced back and was horrified to see the carnage behind him. He quickly realized that he had no hope of reaching the Federal battery. Fearing that a Federal counterattack could completely destroy his already weakened left, exposing the entire line and train to the full brunt of the Union forces, he ordered his men to fall back.

As Duncan began to pursue the fleeing Confederates, he ordered Hall to limber the cannon and advance about three hundred yards, where it could more effectively fire on the fleeing Texans. To support this advance, Duncan drew his left farther and farther from the forces now

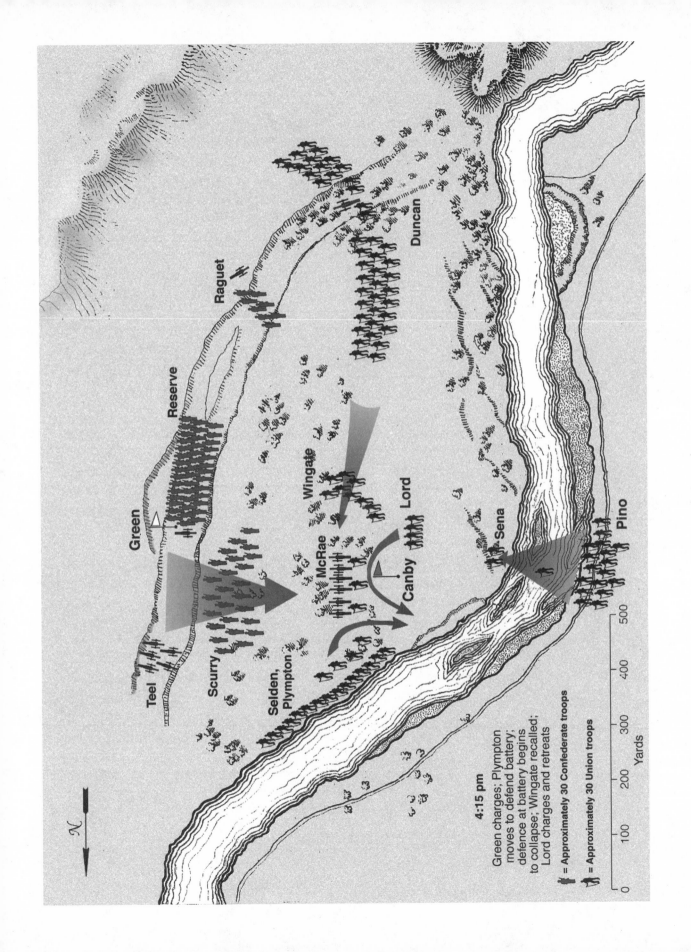

4:15 pm

Green charges; Plympton
moves to defend battery;
defence at battery begins
to collapse; Wingate recalled;
Lord charges and retreats

= Approximately 30 Confederate troops

= Approximately 30 Union troops

Teel

Scurry

Selden,
Plympton

Green

Reserve

Raguet

Wingate

McRae

Canby

Lord

Duncan

Sena

Pino

Yards

0   100   200   300   400   500

N

echelon attack. There would be three waves: 200 men in the first, 250 men in the second, and a final group of 300. Charles Scott of Company A of the Seventh recalled Colonel Green's final words: "Boys, I want Colonel Canby's guns! When I yell, raise the Rebel yell and follow me!"[17]

Once again, the commanders and their subalterns checked up and down the line. Everyone was ready. It was now or never, and with the words, "Up, boys, and at'em!" the first wave leapt forward. Quickly clearing the sand embankment, they charged, screaming like banshees, toward the Federal artillery. Armed as they were with a motley collection of short-range shotguns, fowling pieces, and pistols, their officers had no doubt told them to hold their fire until they were within killing range of their enemy.

Immediately behind the first wave came the second, led by Captains Leseur, Hardeman, and Crosson.[18] As soon as that group had moved out thirty or forty yards, the remaining wave joined the assault.

A Few Minutes after 4:00 P.M., February 21, 1862, Confederate Left

As Confederate commander on the left, Raguet was acutely aware of the vulnerability of his position. Mired in the action to his front, he could only speculate on Green's work a half-mile to the north. His focus was on saving the left. If he failed and the left collapsed, success by Green on the right would make little difference.

Pulling back behind the embankment, he ordered his force, depleted by a number of men who simply kept on running into the sand hills, to form a line of defense between the oncoming Federals, now preparing to resume their advance, and the train to his rear. In a further effort to slow the Union advance, Raguet ordered Reily's mountain howitzer, the last functional piece of artillery left under his control, to take a position between the advancing Federals and the train. Dug in and desperate, he awaited the inevitable Federal onslaught.

9

The Field Is Lost

4:00 P.M., February 21, 1862, McRae's Battery

THE MEN OF COMPANY G OF THE SECOND U.S. CAVALRY AND Company I of the Third U.S. Cavalry, who had been merged in November of 1861 to form McRae's battery, were mostly young and inexperienced. There may have been a few veterans who had experienced pitched battles during the Mexican War, but the only combat most of these soldiers had seen was an occasional Indian raid. Certainly, the men of Mortimore's and Hubbell's volunteer companies had never seen combat on the scale of Valverde.

Canby, astride "Old Chas" in the gap between the battery and the line of support forces about twenty yards to his rear, was the first to spot the Texan charge. Wheeling his horse and galloping to the riverbank, he roused Plympton's battalion and the New Mexico Volunteers and ordered them forward. At the same time, he sent a courier down the line with orders to reinforce the battery's right flank. Roberts, about one hundred yards to the right of the battery, also detected the Texan charge and dispatched Lieutenant Meinhold to Lord and Wingate with similar orders.

As the support forces moved forward from the sanctuary of the riverbank, they saw, stark in the late afternoon shadows, a semicircle of determined Texans almost half a mile long, trotting headlong toward them, elbow to elbow, screaming, shouting, and firing shotguns, muskets, and pistols, seemingly oblivious to the shell and canister that McRae's gunners were ramming home as fast as they could. Massed assaults of this type were common in the larger battles in the East later in the War; but in 1862, in the New Mexico Territory, such an event was unprecedented.

Since the muskets of the New Mexicans were relatively ineffective at ranges greater than a few hundred yards, their first few volleys had little apparent effect. Similarly, since the Texans dove to the ground when they saw the muzzle flashes of the artillery, it too was relatively ineffective for the first two or three rounds, although it may have appeared to some that Texans were dropping like flies:

> watching the flash from the guns, each man threw himself on the ground. . . no wonder they thought we fell in hundreds.[1]

In addition, the efficiency of the Union forces at reloading and firing almost certainly decreased as the Texans continued to approach. Apparently unharmed and certainly undeterred, they must have unnerved the inexperienced New Mexicans.

In the first two or three minutes of the assault on McRae's battery, the Union troops probably fired four or five artillery rounds from each gun and about the same number of rounds from their rifles and muskets.[2] Meanwhile, the Texans had moved two-thirds of the distance from the sandbank and were now beginning to infiltrate the copse of trees on the right and fire effectively with their small arms on the men defending the battery. To make matters even worse, the position of the battery was, as characterized by Lieutenant Bell, "disadvantageous for free operation—crowded and hampered, making a change of front, should the occasion arise, almost impossible."[3]

According to Teel, it took about eight minutes for the Texans to reach the battery. This is consistent with a seven to eight hundred yard movement at ninety to one hundred paces per minute.[4] Ideally, in that time McRae would have been able to get off between eight and sixteen rounds from each piece. Considering the level of training and experience of the artillerymen and their support personnel, and the intensity of the attack, it is unlikely that this rate of fire was maintained. However, the Union fire took its toll and Texans began to fall. There is no question that the Texans absorbed heavier casualties as they got closer and closer to the source of the shell and canister.[5] For example, Marinus van den Heuvel, a former Belgian lancer, was killed by a shot through the left eye while leading Company G of the Fourth Texas (the so-called Dutch Company) in the charge.[6]

The shock value of a frontal assault, particularly on inexperienced troops, was well known to veterans who had seen it used to advantage in the Mexican War.[7] A Union prisoner, captured during a charge on an

and Crosson's companies captured several men from the Colorado Volunteers and the U.S. Tenth Infantry (including its captain, George Rossell).[20] During this second wave, McRae's subaltern, Lyman Mishler, was shot through the chest "while ramming the last charge into one of his pieces."[21] At the same time, a Texas officer, perhaps a former comrade in arms, is said to have shouted, "Surrender, McRae, we don't want to kill you!" to which the North Carolinian replied, "I shall never forsake my guns!"[22] Lewis Roe of Rockwell's Company F of the Seventh recalled that, during the charge, "I heard no orders, no shouting, no yelling. Everyone was busy fighting."[23]

It was during this melee that McRae fell with a fatal bullet wound to the head (some say he was shot by Lockridge). It has also been reported in more romantic accounts of the battle that McRae, hearing Lockridge's original comment, shouted, "Shoot the son-of-a-bitch!" and that they died almost simultaneously with "their blood mingling" on the barrel of the contested piece.[24]

The fight for the battery had gone on for several minutes when Wingate's winded troops, recalled from the right at the double quick, came within range of the charging Texans. The four companies halted about sixty yards away and poured a concentrated fire into the Confederate flank. Lord's men of the First Cavalry had gotten within about twenty yards of the battery when Wingate opened fire. Seeing that he would soon be seriously exposed to "friendly fire," Lord ordered, "Dismount and prepare to fight on foot!"

The troopers quickly gave their horses to the assigned handlers and moved back a few yards to the protection of the riverbank, from which they again began to fire on the Texans who had overrun McRae's position.

For a moment, it seemed as if the men of the Fifth Infantry might have saved the day. However, Captain Wingate was badly wounded by an artillery round and the Confederates were quickly reinforced and came on again.[25]

4:15 P.M., February 21, 1862, West Bank at the Middle Ford

Colonel Miguel Pino's men had escorted the ammunition train from Fort Craig to the battlefield in the middle of the afternoon. Canby had ordered Pino to remain in reserve on the west bank, pending a decision on the Federal course of action, so the seven companies were anxiously awaiting orders when they first heard the dull thuds of McRae's cannons opening up on the Texans' position.

Positioned as they were on the west bank, with cottonwoods on both sides obscuring their view of the field, the men of the Second New Mexico Volunteers could not have seen the Texans leap from behind the sandbank. Because they were almost a mile from the start of the Confederate charge, they would have only heard the crash of musketry and the deep booming of the artillery, perhaps punctuated by a faint Rebel yell or shouted Federal command. As the Texans neared McRae's battery, these men from northern New Mexico, who had not yet received their first real taste of battle, saw the clouds of smoke and dust further obscure their view of the activities across the river.

Suddenly, figures began to appear, running out of the smoke toward the ford: first singly, then several at a time—volunteers, regulars, and loose and terrified horses—all fleeing from the fury of the battlefield. Against this backdrop, Canby's couriers arrived, desperately pleading with the men to ford the river and reinforce the battery at the double quick. Company B, under the command of Captain José D. Sena, and part of another plunged across the river, but others were less enthusiastic, despite cajoling and threats from Pino and the other officers.[26]

Back on the east bank, even the men who had stubbornly defended the battery realized that it was a lost cause. Private Daniel Robinson of the Seventh U. S. Infantry recalled:

> Men were breaking to the rear and I thought of the low bank from which we had deployed. . . . I broke for the bank and to my surprise found it was quite steep and I was up to my waist in water . . . quite a number of men were under it, unsure whether they should cross [the river] or remain.[27]

Canby had gotten a taste of the intensity himself. He had Old Chas shot out from under him during the charge, and he is said to have picked up a musket and continued to exhort the men forward.[28] He now was forced to admit that Pino, Lord, and Wingate would not be enough. Realizing that Duncan would be unable to provide reinforcements for several minutes and seeing that further attempts to recapture the battery would be futile, he reluctantly dispatched a courier to Duncan. Then he turned to the bugler at his side and ordered him to sound "Retreat."

Passing along the riverbank, he personally ordered Lord to mount and retreat across the river.

4:00 P.M., February 21, 1862, Union Right Wing

Major Duncan and the Federal troops on the Union right had watched as the Texans (under Raguet) retreated behind the sand embankments. Sensing an advantage, he ordered Carson, Graydon, and Ingraham to anchor the Federal position to the left of Hall's twenty-four-pounder with Treacy's Company D of the Third Cavalry placed on the far left. Meanwhile, he repositioned four companies—Morris, Howland, and Tilford's dismounted troopers from the Third Cavalry and Brotherton's company of the Fifth Infantry—to the right of the twenty-four-pounder. As the infantry wheeled into position, he ordered Hall to limber the gun and advance up the dry riverbed to a position from which he could finally begin to enfilade the Texans' tenuous position.

Just as Hall's howitzer was beginning to move, Canby's courier galloped up with the information that McRae's battery had fallen and passed to Duncan the order to disengage and retreat to the fort. Reluctantly, Duncan ordered the bugler to sound the retreat. He dispatched messengers to Carson and Treacy on his left, informing them of Canby's orders.

Duncan's courier arrived at Carson's position within a few minutes. Carson, unaware of the misfortune on the Union left, received the order with some chagrin. However, an order was an order, and Carson directed his bugler to sound "Retreat," and the eight companies of volunteers, together with the regulars commanded by Ingraham and Treacy, fell back to the bosque east of the lower ford, which had been so hotly contested in the morning's fighting.

There, they joined Duncan and his regulars and forded the river unchallenged. By about five o'clock, the cold, wet, dispirited Federal forces were mustered on the western bank and began the long march back to Fort Craig where they arrived at about seven that evening.

On the way to the right, another courier found Captain Selden with the four companies (B, D, F, and I) of the Fifth Infantry and the wounded Wingate to the right of the battery. Selden was told to fall back slowly, covering the movement of the rest of the Union forces to the middle ford and across the river. Dispatching a squad to carry their fallen hero

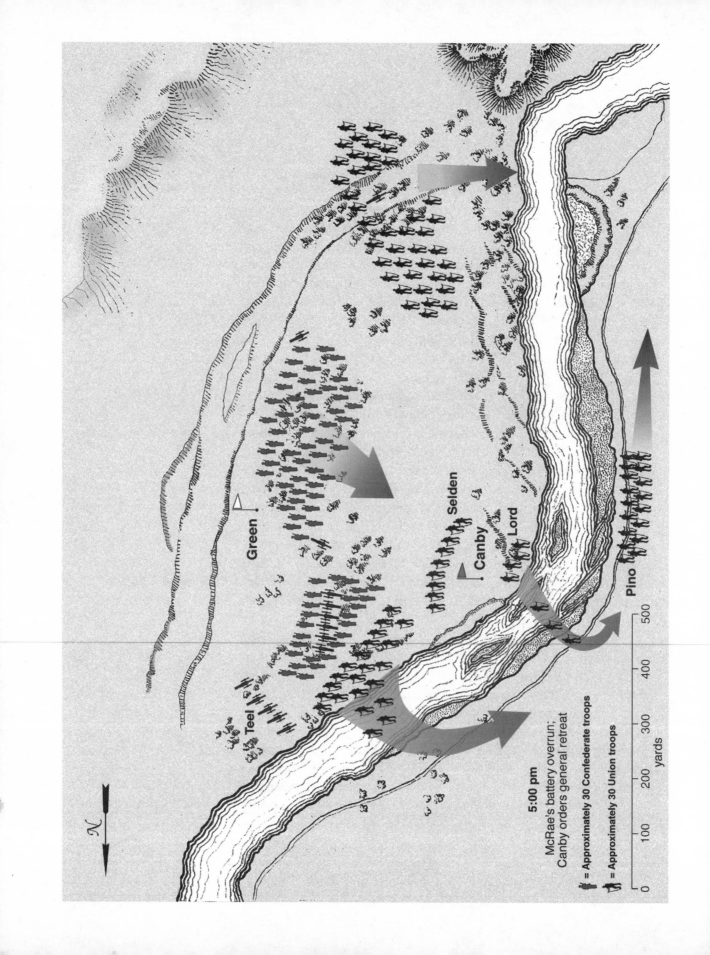

5:00 pm

McRae's battery overrun;
Canby orders general retreat

🐎 = Approximately 30 Confederate troops

🐎 = Approximately 30 Union troops

Green

Teel

Selden

Canby

Lord

Pino

N

0   100   200   300   400   500

yards

plaintive, "Please don't shoot me anymore!" Looking down, he saw a wounded Union soldier, barely able to keep his head above the water. Dropping his own gun, he waded into the cold river and pulled the man to safety.[7]

Late Evening, February 21, 1862, Fort Craig Hospital

Chief Surgeon Joseph Bill, his assistant Basil Norris, and their staff had never been faced with a situation like the one they now confronted. The more than 160 wounded officers and men, mutilated in every conceivable manner, so overwhelmed the small infirmary that satellite "hospitals" were set up in the officers' and company quarters.[8] At least five of the wounded required immediate amputations, and the stench and moans in the "wards" must have been overpowering. Virtually all of the mattresses in the fort were commandeered, and medical supplies, including lint muslin, stretchers, dressings, and pulveris licii, were all but exhausted.[9]

Periodically, men would wander through the makeshift wards, searching for a comrade, hoping against hope that he was still alive. Ickis reports searching through the room "where the dead are piled up," looking for Private Harrison Berry of the Colorado Volunteers.[10]

Chaos reigned inside the fort. The men from the volunteers and militia regiments, who had camped outside the walls, were now crowded inside, together with the pack animals, cavalry mounts, and the beef herd. The compound, designed to hold three hundred men and their families, now held nearly ten times that number.

Canby and his officers had no real idea of their actual "effectives." Their best guess was that about two hundred men had been killed or wounded and that perhaps another hundred or so were missing and presumed to have deserted. Although Canby bravely said that the loss of these deserters "added to rather than diminished" his strength, he must have had some second thoughts.[11] Had the missing men run away, or had they gone over to the Texans? And what about their ammunition and horses—were these now in Sibley's camp?

In view of the situation, and with a particular concern about the danger posed by the captured Federal artillery, Canby kept the garrison at the ready. He dispatched Major Donaldson north, with about 280 militiamen under Colonel Nicholas Pino, under cover of darkness and with orders to "remove or destroy any public property that might fall into the hands of the enemy." In addition, he initiated a plan to place Lieutenant Colonel Manuel Chavez in command of some of the volunteers, including several men from Chacón's and Deus's companies, as partisans "for the purpose of operating on the flanks of the enemy."[12] In particular, this hand-picked crew was tasked with denying Sibley any "resources" as he marched north.[13]

Canby made several visits to the hospital wards, attempting to shore up the spirits of the injured men. On one of these visits, he visited the badly wounded Captain Wingate, whose leg "was torn to pieces from the knee down."[14] One member of the Fifth Infantry later reported that during this visit Wingate, furious at Canby's withdrawal from the battery, accused Canby of being a traitor: "Leave me! You are a traitor! If I could but get to Washington!"[15] Wingate would linger in pain until June 1, when he died of complications of the leg wound. It was also reported that Colorado Chaplain Lewis Hamilton castigated Canby for being a traitor and was placed in custody for a few hours.[16]

Although the number of casualties was probably the major cause, part of the Federal morale problem and the accusations of Canby's lack of battlefield fortitude no doubt stemmed from the persistent but unfounded rumor that Canby and Sibley were brothers-in-law.[17]

February 22, 1862, Valverde Battlefield

On Washington's Birthday, 1862, Brigadier General Henry Hopkins Sibley and his victorious Texans camped on the battlefield of Valverde. The Confederate dead were hurriedly buried in graves near the sand hills, and the wounded were stabilized sufficiently to permit them to be moved to the field hospital that was to be established in Socorro, about thirty miles to the north. Private Smith, assigned to a burial detail, described the process: "We dug a ditch four feet deep, wrapped 40 of our boys in their blankets, and placed them in the earth without so much as marking the spot."[18]

Lieutenant Colonel Sutton, erstwhile leader of the Seventh Texas Mounted Volunteers, was informed that his only hope of survival was amputation of his mutilated leg, but said that he "did not intend to hobble 'round the balance of his days on one leg and that when his leg went that he would go with it!"[19] He died on February 22, in camp, on the field of Valverde. One of the Texans described his interment:

Graves at Valverde as sketched by A. B. Peticolas. Courtesy the family.

> It was the most impressive funeral I ever witnessed. A detachment of his command with arms reversed followed his remains in silence to the grave. All was silence profound—not a word was spoken, not a gun fired—no sound was heard but the chilling rattle of the sod as it was thrown on the body of our lost colonel. 'Farewell, Gallant Eagle, thou art buried in light!...Godspeed thee to heaven, lost star of our night'[20]

The solemnity of the day was further punctuated by the faint echoes of the salutatory musket salvos from the Fort Craig cemetery as the Union dead were also laid to rest with military honors.[21]

Together, Sibley, Green, and the other Confederate officers took stock of their situation. Not certain of the condition of the Federal army and recognizing the potential danger of his situation, Sibley decided on one last ploy before moving north. Under a white flag, he dispatched Captain Shannon and the newly breveted Colonel Scurry with an escort of ten men through the picket line on the west bank to ride to Fort Craig. About an hour later, the small group was met just outside the walls of the fort and escorted inside by "a guard of 18 Mexicans with a Dutch sergeant and an Irish corporal."[22]

Taken to Canby, Scurry presented a short note from Sibley introducing the two officers and noting that they would represent his "views and purposes."[23] Those views and purposes amounted to a demand that Canby surrender Fort Craig to the Confederate army. Not surprisingly, Canby refused and sent the Texas contingent back to Sibley with instructions that if the Confederates wanted the fort, they would have to take it. Scurry noted the outer ditches and strong fortifications and sug-

to Sibley that taking the fort would not be an easy task. Considering the state of their ammunition, provisions, and livestock, the Confederates decided to break camp and move north.

After Scurry's visit, Chacón and Graydon escorted carts to the battle-field to retrieve more of the dead and wounded, including the body of the gallant McRae. Chacón was moved by the carnage: "The field was covered with blood, horses, torn and dismembered limbs, and heads separated from their bodies—a spectacle that was horrible." He also noted that "it was a great pleasure for us to see the chivalry and courtesy with which we [the Union and Texas contingents] treated each other, forget-ting the anger and antagonisms of yesterday in the solemn presence of the dead." This mortuary detail also removed Bascom's body from a sand bar in the middle of the river.[24]

In a published announcement, Colonel Canby specified that formal military honors would be rendered to the dead of Valverde in a four-company infantry battalion parade with a firing party of one battery of artillery at 9:00 A.M. on the twenty-fifth. He further asked that all the men pray that "He who tempers the wind to the shorn lamb will deal tenderly with the bereaved relations and friends of the brave dead."[25]

When the sun set on February 21, 1862, the Sibley Brigade was un-questionably the victor on the field of Valverde. Colonel Canby and about twenty-five hundred of his troops were retreating to Fort Craig, and the Texans had captured six of the eight pieces of Federal artillery and dam-aged a seventh. However, once the flush of the battle had subsided, the Confederate commanders must have had a few second thoughts about their "victory." For one thing, they had suffered 229 casualties (71 dead or mortally wounded, 157 wounded, and 1 prisoner), a 10 percent casu-alty rate on the field, one of the highest battlefield casualty rates in North America to that time. And among the casualties were several key offic-ers: Samuel Lockridge, John Sutton, Marinus van den Heuvel, dead on the field; and Tom Green, Willis Lang, Henry Raguet, Demetrius Bass, Trevanion Teel, and D. A. Hubbard, all wounded.

Another "casualty" of Valverde may well have been Sibley himself. Though his penchant for the bottle was well known, his retirement from the field when the battle was being lost, especially in the light of Green's success in "turning it around," did not go unnoticed by the troops.

Peticolas said that the old general was "heartily despised by every man in the brigade for his want of feeling, poor generalship, and cowardice."[26]

Another of his soldiers noted that, "the Commanding General was an old army officer whose love for liquor exceeded that for home, country, or God,"[27] and yet another assailed "certain persons" who "stay in comfortable quarters...soaking up rum and whiskey while others are doing the work."[28]

In fact, Sibley never again led his brigade in battle in New Mexico; he stayed in Albuquerque during the Battle of Glorieta, in Los Lunas during the skirmish at Peralta, and in his ambulance during the ignominious retreat through the San Mateo Mountains.

In addition to their human casualties, the Texans had lost the 160 mules on the night of the twentieth, many more horses and mules during the fight on the twenty-first, and thirty wagons (about 20 percent of their train) on the evening of the twenty-first. In fact, because of the casualties in horseflesh, the entire Fourth Texas Mounted Volunteers "voluntarily" became an infantry regiment and conducted the rest of the New Mexico campaign on foot.

The food and supplies from Fort Craig, which had been one goal of this phase of the invasion, were intact and in Union hands. Thus, Sibley and his men were forced to continue to "live off the land" as they turned north. This presented a challenge, particularly for forage for the remaining animals, since it was in the middle of a New Mexico winter and on the heels of two years of drought. Because they had to commandeer food and forage from the local populations, they left resentment in their wake instead of the hoped-for recruitment to their cause.

Thus, the morale of the Texans was a mixed bag as they marched away from Valverde on February 23. The ferocity of the battle must have given even the battle-seasoned veterans pause. Despite the apparent inexperience of the New Mexico Volunteers, the Texans moved north with the certain knowledge that over three thousand armed (and now somewhat battle-hardened) men remained between them and home. In addition, the hoped-for allegiance of the New Mexico population had failed to materialize. In fact, Sibley and his men discovered that, although there was no particular love lost between some New Mexicans and the Union, most Hispanics truly hated the so-called Texians. The army was one of outcasts, moving farther away from friendly territory in a cold, uninviting New Mexico winter.

Colonel William Steele, writing to Richmond from Mesilla in the middle of March, summed up the dreary picture. Sibley, he declared, was

> cut off from mail; not well supplied with either ammunition or provisions...a strong force at Fort Craig in his rear...his army in the midst of a population of 80,000 souls possessing no very friendly spirit towards us...in a country nearly or quite exhausted as regards forage and other army supplies...a spirit of insubordination and prejudice against General Sibley himself that goes so far as to accuse him of deliberate plans to deliver his command into the hands of our enemies.[29]

This state of affairs was "adjusted" by Richmond politicians, however, and on April 5, Confederate Secretary of State Judah Benjamin noted Sibley's "rout of the enemy forces at Valverde" in a communiqué to James Mason, the Confederate States' ambassador to the Court of Saint James. Further, on April 16 the Confederate Congress passed a resolution of thanks to Sibley for his "complete and brilliant victories achieved over our enemies in New Mexico."[30]

Sibley's woes notwithstanding, Canby and his men were far from "tall clover." By virtue of his tactical withdrawal, Canby had minimized his losses. He initially estimated his losses at 284 (61 dead, 127 wounded, and 96 missing). However, as the days wore on, the numbers grew alarmingly. When the final totals were made, the Union casualties stood at about 475 (111 dead, 160 wounded, and 204 missing), about 17 percent of the approximately 2,800 troops he had brought to the ford. The heaviest casualty rates were suffered around McRae's battery, including Rockwell's company at 71 percent and Dodd's Coloradans at 56 percent. This must have been truly a shocking experience for the Union troops. In addition, six of Canby's eight cannons had been captured and one of the two remaining guns was damaged, leaving Sibley with a significant advantage in artillery. The Union forces had lost five key officers (the North Carolina artilleryman Alexander McRae, Maine-born Roderic Stone, Pennsylvanian Lyman Mishler, the experienced Indian fighter George Bascom, and the former Irish enlistee George McDermott), and Benjamin Wingate was mortally wounded.

In retrospect, Canby was no doubt convinced that his pre-battle assessment of the volunteers had been correct. He blamed them for the loss of the battle and was acutely aware that they constituted nearly 70 percent of his reserves at Fort Craig. In fact, the problem worsened between the twenty-first and twenty-eighth when Captain Saturnino Barrientos of the Fifth New Mexico Volunteers deserted with his entire company.[31]

Canby thought so little of the militia that he actually dismissed most of them, sending some north with Major Donaldson on the night of the twenty-first, some with Wesche on the night of the twenty-second, and simply letting others go home.

The likelihood of substantive reinforcements from the East was not good; lack of money to pay the troops had already resulted in a small mutiny; and a force of nearly twenty-five hundred proven fighters was between him and the heartland of New Mexico. So Canby saw himself outmanned and outgunned as he huddled behind the walls of Fort Craig, probably hoping that Sibley would not take up his challenge and attack the fort. Based on some reports, he may even have had his carpenters make some "Quaker Cannons" (large logs carved so as to appear to be artillery from a distance) to at least give a semblance of more substantial defenses at the fort.[32]

Considering his options, Canby decided that if Sibley moved north he and his force should remain at Fort Craig rather than pursue. He and the other senior officers felt that by remaining in the south he could intercept any Texas reinforcements and that the combination of Federal forces in the north, the destruction of military supplies in Albuquerque and Santa Fe, and the work of his newly created band of partisans would eventually take its toll on the Valverde-weakened Sibley Brigade.

Governor Connelly also must have been dispirited, not least because his hacienda at Los Pinos (now Bosque Farms) lay directly between Sibley and his objectives in the north.[33] Leaving surreptitiously on the night of the twenty-fifth[34] and skirting well to the west to avoid the Texans, Connelly rode north with a few militia officers and the newly constituted guerrilla forces under Lieutenant Colonel Valdez, pausing in Los Pinos only long enough to warn his foreman of the potential problem and to distribute his cattle, merchandise, and equipment to the people of Peralta and Los Pinos to prevent its seizure by the Texans. Moving on to Santa Fe, he ordered the territorial government to pack up and move to Las Vegas, where nearby Fort Union could offer some measure of protection from the invaders.[35]

The first reports of Valverde reached the rest of the Colorado Volunteers in Denver on March 1. The report was a call to arms: "Dodd's company has been killed to a man by the Texans!" Although exaggerated,[36] the report galvanized the men of Colorado, and within two days they were on the road south with vengeance on their minds. This mood prevailed, and perhaps even intensified, until the climactic face-off at Glorieta on March 28.

11

Retrospective

ALTHOUGH THIS BOOK HAS FOCUSED ON THE BATTLE OF VALVERDE, it is appropriate to at least summarize the rest of Sibley's ill-fated New Mexico campaign.

The Texans broke camp at Valverde at about noon on February 23. Because of their loss of animals, they were forced to burn some "saddles and old clothes" before leaving to prevent Canby from capturing them.[1] Heading north past the village of Valverde, the army sacked a store at the ranch of Robert H. Stapleton, a colonel in the New Mexico Militia at Fort Craig. According to Peticolas, three thousand dollars worth of merchandise was confiscated and distributed to Sibley's army.[2]

Although the bulk of the force remained in camp near Stapleton's Ranch, a contingent kept moving north and captured Socorro, on the night of February 23, with essentially no resistance. Sibley elected to leave the seriously wounded men from Valverde in a hospital there.[3] A small contingent under Captain A. S. Thurmond was dispatched about sixty miles west to Cubero, where they captured the Federal ammunition depot and its supply of about sixty small arms and three thousand rounds of ammunition on March 3.

The main Confederate force entered Albuquerque on March 7, where they discovered that Assistant Quartermaster Herbert Enos, following Canby's orders, had fired the supply depot before abandoning the post. The Texans' advance party arrived in Santa Fe on March 13, where they paused for a few days.

Determined to press northward to Fort Union, Sibley dispatched two columns: one left Albuquerque on March 21, and the other left Santa Fe on March 25. Unbeknownst to the Texans, the First Regiment of Colorado Volunteers, commanded by Colonel John Slough and spurred on by the exaggerated rumors of Dodd's demise at Valverde, had reached

Fort Union in record time by virtue of a twelve-day, four-hundred-mile forced march from Denver via a wintry Raton Pass. Unwilling to wait for Canby's orders, some of the Coloradans continued south and engaged the Confederates in battle at the mouth of Apache Canyon on March 26.

The fight was continued on March 28, with both sides reinforced in what came to be known as the Battle of Glorieta, sometimes described as "the Gettysburg of the West." Once again the Texans left their train inadequately protected, and this time they lost it all. In an unanticipated flank attack by a battalion of Coloradans and regulars under the "Mad Methodist," Major John Chivington, Union forces burned about seventy wagons and killed or drove off five to six hundred mules at Johnson's Ranch.[4] Although the battle itself was another Texas tactical victory, the Texans knew that the loss of their logistical support, coupled with the approach of Canby's army from Fort Craig, had doomed the invasion. Having abandoned Santa Fe on April 12, they left Albuquerque in retreat.[5]

After a brief skirmish at Governor Connelly's hacienda near Peralta on April 15 and a disastrous week-long trek around the San Mateo Mountains to avoid another fight at Fort Craig, a demoralized and diminished brigade of Texans straggled back into the Mesilla Valley around the first of May, ending the Confederate invasion of New Mexico.

Given the battered, bloodied, and disheveled status of his army, it is interesting to note that Sibley still maintained that his retreating brigade had "beaten the enemy at every encounter and against large odds."[6] Perhaps he had been at the bottle again as he drafted the letter!

Sibley's view of the value of New Mexico had also taken a radical turn. Far from the glowing descriptions given to Jeff Davis in July, Sibley's parting description of the territory was a place "not worth a quarter of the blood and treasure expended in its conquest."[7] He further noted that the complaints of the people against the Apaches and Navajos in the territory were such that he had encouraged the people to "legalize the enslaving of them."

From the Mesilla Valley and Fort Bliss the army limped back to San Antonio, arriving there during the summer of 1862 with fewer than eighteen hundred of the twenty-six hundred who had so confidently headed north from Fort Thorn in February.

Despite the failure of the New Mexico campaign, the Sibley Brigade's participation in the Civil War was far from over. The general led the men into Louisiana, where he once again ran afoul of both the bottle and his superior officers. Sibley was relieved of his command in early 1863 by General Richard Taylor, son of the former president Zachary Taylor. Despite the loss of its namesake, the brigade continued to fight for the Confederacy in Louisiana and along the Red River under the leadership of Tom Green. McRae's cannons, christened "the Valverde Battery" and commanded by future Texas governor Joseph Draper Sayers, now served as a rallying point for all of these troops and were a centerpiece of the brigade until its final disbandment in Texas at the end of the war.[8]

The Battle of Valverde was fought not just by companies and regiments but by men, many of whom went on to further fame or infamy. The besotted Confederate visionary, Henry Hopkins Sibley, along with several other high-ranking Civil War veterans, went to Egypt after the war to help organize the Egyptian army under Khedive Ismail. Again a victim of his own intemperance, Sibley returned to the U.S. in 1873 and died, forgotten and in poverty, in Fredericksburg, Virginia, in 1886.

Tom Green, the fighting lawyer from La Grange, Texas, led the brigade in its fights along the Red River until he was killed by an artillery round on April 12, 1864, while leading an attack on three federal gunboats near Blair's Landing, Louisiana. William "Dirty Shirt" Scurry was promoted to full colonel following Valverde and to brigadier general on September 12, 1863. He was killed during the Battle of Jenkins Ferry on April 30, 1864.

Trevanion Teel fought out the war as a Confederate artillery officer, then settled in El Paso to practice law. In 1889, he returned to Albuquerque and helped locate and unearth eight of Sibley's cannons that had been hastily buried in a corral during the Texans' retreat. Teel died in Ysleta, Texas, in 1899. Major Henry Raguet, leader of Green's critical afternoon diversionary attack on Hall's battery, was killed while leading his troops during the Battle of Glorieta on March 28, 1862, and was remembered by Colonel Reily as "a man without reproach, a soldier without fear."[9]

On the Union side, Colonel Canby was transferred to Washington, D.C., in September 1862. He later served as commander of New York

City and of the Military Division of the West Mississippi during the final battles around Mobile. He returned to the west after the war as a major general and was killed on April 11, 1873, by a Modoc Indian named "Cap'n Jack" during pacification efforts in eastern Oregon, becoming the only general officer killed during the Indian Wars.[10]

Thomas Duncan, the man Lieutenant Colonel Roberts accused of costing him a morning victory, had part of his skull shot away by a cannonball during the skirmish at Albuquerque on April 8, 1862, but recovered from his wounds, was breveted to brigadier general for his service during the New Mexico campaign, and died in Washington, D.C., in 1887.[11]

Benjamin Wingate, near-hero of the attempts to recapture the battery, died of his wounds on June 1 at Fort Craig. Fort Fauntleroy, near present-day Gallup, New Mexico, was renamed Fort Wingate in his honor.[12] Henry Selden, Wingate's immediate superior at Valverde, was promoted to major and died of complications of a cold in February 1865, while in command of Fort Union. Fort Selden, near Doña Ana, New Mexico, was named in his honor.

Benjamin Roberts, near-victor at Valverde, was promoted to colonel on the day following the battle and was eventually promoted to major general of volunteers because of his gallantry at the battles of Cedar Mountain and Second Manassas. After the war, he taught military science at Yale University and invented and marketed a new breech-loading rifle. He died in Washington, D.C., in 1875 and is buried in his hometown of Manchester, Vermont.

Robert Hall, whose twenty-four-pounders nearly carried the day on the Union right, was severely wounded near Petersburg, Virginia, in 1864, but he recovered and was eventually promoted to brigadier general, serving with distinction during the Spanish American War.[13]

Kit Carson remained in New Mexico and led several expeditions against the Apaches and Navajos, including the 1864 raid on Canyon de Chelly. He died a brevet brigadier general in Boggsville, Colorado, on May 23, 1868.

The valiant Alexander McRae was interred at Fort Craig until 1867, when his remains were transferred to the cemetery at West Point. A military outpost south of Fort Craig on the edge of the Jornada del Muerto was named Fort McRae in his honor.[14]

Colonel Gabriel Paul, left at Fort Craig during the Battle of Valverde, was also left at Fort Union during the Battle of Glorieta by the flamboyant John Slough of Colorado. Paul would lose his sight at Gettysburg and be breveted to brigadier general for his work in that battle. He died on May 5, 1886.

Fort Craig continued to serve as a southern bastion for Union forces in New Mexico until its abandonment and sale to the Valverde Land and Irrigation Company, in 1894, for the princely sum of $1,070.50 (including 50 cents for a chicken house and $4.00 for a water closet!). For years all that remained of Fort Craig were a few crumbling adobe walls off a dirt road in Socorro County. However, the site is now owned by the Bureau of Land Management with open access, and Congress has appropriated money to construct a visitor center.

Having the benefit of over 130 years of analysis and hindsight to draw upon, I conclude that the outcome of the Battle of Valverde was largely dictated by a combination of five factors: personalities; strategy and tactics; logistics and organization; troop behavior and experience; and terrain.

Personalities.

Colonel Edward R. S. Canby was a conservative, by-the-book soldier who consistently overestimated his foe; who mistrusted the bulk of his own troops; and who was accustomed to proceeding "with all deliberate speed." In fact, General Ulysses S. Grant would later characterize him as "deliberate in all his work" and as "an exceedingly modest soldier who served out the war, in large part, behind a desk but he was positive that it was Canby's superior efficiency in that capacity which kept him there."[15]

At Valverde, when he saw minimal hope for complete victory, Canby opted to cut his losses and retreat. He clearly felt that the loss of McRae's battery gave the Texans a substantial advantage in artillery and that this issue overrode the potential of Duncan's forces on the right to roll up the Texan left and capture their train. He also clearly felt (correctly, as it turned out) that he would be the ultimate victor in the inevitable war of attrition, regardless of any single day's battlefield performance.

Green and Scurry, on the other hand, were more daring, albeit driven in that direction by somewhat more desperate circumstances. The fortuitous combination of the two sequential charges—Raguet on the left followed by Scurry on the right—was an audacious move with significant risk: both assaults were made into the teeth of powerful artillery and with an assumption of poor odds. In addition, if either were seriously repulsed, the entire brigade could be open to an immediate flanking maneuver with devastating consequences. Yet the charges were ordered and the risk accepted.

Strategy and Tactics.

Sibley had decided that a frontal assault on Fort Craig would be futile, so he attempted to split Canby's forces by simultaneous moves at the fort and the ford. By pinning a substantial fraction of Canby's army at the fort, Sibley hoped to obtain both a numerical and an artillery advantage at the ford, since Canby would undoubtedly leave some of his cannons at Fort Craig (as he did until the early forenoon), even if he sent a sizable force to Valverde. In addition, Sibley, aware of the large number of inexperienced New Mexico Volunteers and militiamen in the Union contingent, probably thought that he could also achieve a significant advantage by forcing Canby to split up his regulars.

The loss of a substantial portion of the draft animals on the night of the twentieth derailed part of Sibley's plans and forced him to move his entire force to the ford and to forgo the option of pinning down some of Canby's troops at the fort.

After the afternoon of the twentieth, with its failed attempt to attack the Confederate's dry camp, Canby's strategy was one of waiting for Sibley to move and then reacting. However, once the battle was joined on the morning of the twenty-first, the roles reversed, and the Union forces under Roberts took the initiative. Roberts's plan was first to control the lower ford, then to cross the artillery and infantry and roll up the Texas line. When the stubborn Texas resistance stalled the Union attack behind a strong natural defensive barrier in the sandhills, and when Duncan could not be persuaded to attack more vigorously, Roberts retrenched and waited for Canby to arrive.

Canby's late-afternoon plan for victory basically followed Roberts's lead. He chose to anchor his left near the river with McRae's battery and then roll up the Texan's left with Hall's battery and Duncan's forces. Although the plan was sound, Canby made three tactical errors. His first error was to use two companies of inexperienced New Mexico Volunteers, Hubbell and Mortimore, as the principal defenders of McRae's battery and to place Pino's regiment of New Mexico Volunteers as a principal reserve. This choice is particularly surprising in light of Canby's consistent complaints and vocal concerns about the reliability of the New Mexico Volunteers.

Canby's second error was to advance the battery before the supporting forces and reserves were fully manned and prepared to defend the battery. Canby's third error was to allow the placement of the guns in a restrictive and vulnerable position adjacent to a grove of trees that he did not control. This was compounded by the tactical redeployment of his center so far to the right that McRae's right flank was left "in the air." Clearly, these decisions were partially due to an incorrect assumption on Canby's part about the disposition of the Texas forces and may also reflect incomplete communication of intent and timing from Canby to his battalion and artillery commanders—the so-called fog of war.

Green's late-afternoon tactics, born of desperation after losses on his left and the failed lancer charge, represented the first real initiative taken by the Confederates since Scurry's spirited morning fight in the lower bosque. Green's two charges desynchronized the Union advance, split Canby's forces, and resulted in a local numerical advantage on the Confederate right at the north end of the battlefield. Raguet's oblique charge toward Hall's twenty-four-pounder drew Carson, Wingate, and Ingraham away from McRae, opening a gap that Scurry exploited as his classical, multi-echelon assault enveloped the battery.

Logistics and Organization.

Sibley's overall scheme for the New Mexico invasion emphasized force mobility at the expense of logistical support. This proved to be a poor decision almost from the outset. Canby recognized that Sibley's force could not "live off the land," and so his basic approach was one of attrition rather than decisive confrontation. Thus, once McRae's battery had been captured, Canby's decision to abandon the field at Valverde and force Sibley to move north without remounts, forage, or sufficient food was no doubt the correct one. In fact, inadequate attention to logistics proved to be the enemy that cost the Texans the fruits of the victories they won on the battlefield.

On the other hand, Canby's supply situation was far from ideal. He was forced to ration flour after the Battle of Valverde, and men from

Fort Craig were sent far afield to get forage for the animals remaining at the fort. However, he had a source of supplies and identified supply lines that, though temporarily disrupted, could not be permanently denied by the Texans. Thus, on balance, Canby "won" the logistical battle at Valverde, even though he lost the fight itself.

Canby's logistical victory was helped considerably by Sibley's failure to intercept the supply train that arrived at Fort Craig on February 15, bringing much-needed supplies to the Union troops. In addition, the fact that Federal reinforcements continued to arrive as late as February 20 suggests that Sibley's plan for interdicting Canby's logistical support was badly flawed.

Another critical logistical mistake was Sibley's assumption that he would be accepted, indeed even welcomed, by the local populace, thus permitting his army to "live off the land" without generating resentment and hostility. Had the Sibley Brigade been just a Confederate army, this assumption might have been valid. However, the New Mexicans saw them not as Confederates but as Texans, and so historic passions were aroused and the anticipated support evaporated. In fact, Canby and his Union soldiers, though no great heroes to the New Mexicans, were much the lesser of evils when compared with yet another invasion of Texans.[16]

Finally, the Texans were ill prepared for winter marches and a sustained series of pitched battles against well-armed troops. They had a few coats and limited blankets and clearly suffered from the capricious cruelty of the New Mexico winter. In addition, the Sibley Brigade was configured as a "mounted rifles" unit, essentially a lightly armed cavalry force, relying mostly on shotguns, handguns, and very light artillery. They were not equipped to besiege fortifications, and so serious threats against the battlements of Fort Craig and Fort Union were out of the question. Their tactical successes at Valverde and Glorieta are, in fact, testimonials to the bravery of the troops and the skill of the battle leaders rather than to the underlying strength of the force.

Troop Behavior and Experience.

Canby, Roberts, and even some of the Texans attributed the Federal defeat at Valverde to the poor performance of the New Mexico Volunteers. While it is certainly true that some of the men under Hubbell and

Mortimore turned and ran when the Fourth Texas Volunteers charged the battery, it would be incorrect to extrapolate this to make a complete condemnation of the entire New Mexico Volunteer force. In fact, the context in which Hubbell and Mortimore found themselves must be carefully considered before final judgment is rendered.

First, consider the training and experience of the New Mexico Volunteers. Most of the men had been recruited during the fall and early winter of 1861–1862. In the months preceding Valverde what little fighting experience they had was restricted to isolated sorties against the Navajos and Apaches. None of them had ever participated in pitched battles against large masses of trained, well-armed men supported by artillery. With some exceptions, the officer corps was similarly inexperienced.

Although the rank-and-file Texans were also inexperienced, their officers were not. Many had gained experience in fighting in the Mexican War, in the Indian wars, or even in Europe, and they had been together since the middle of the summer and had done little else but train and march since that time. In addition, they were probably better motivated, not only in a strategic sense but also tactically. Recall that most of the men had gone without water since they left the river at Paraje on the nineteenth. The sight of the Rio Grande gleaming in the distance must have been a powerful incentive.

The bulk of the New Mexico Volunteers (and, indeed, the bulk of the territory's population) felt no particular loyalty to the United States. "Washington City" was a far-off place, and issues of state's rights and slavery were not significant in the lives of most of the men. They had joined the army because of promises of money (much of which had not been forthcoming) and to protect their homes from the depredations of marauding Indians. In addition, there was residual resentment of the "Texians" that dated to the ill-fated invasions of New Mexico in the 1840s.

On balance, the New Mexico Volunteers appeared to have performed adequately during the course of the battle. Certainly some of the groups (Graydon, Chacón, Sena, and Carson) performed quite admirably. Valdez and Graydon participated throughout the day as a part of Duncan's battalion on the right. Carson's companies were thrown into action in the mid-afternoon and fired a part of the devastating volley that helped to foil Raguet's attack on Hall. Chacón and Deus were used by Canby in his "demonstration" south of Fort Craig on the sixteenth. Wesche led a group of militiamen against three Confederate companies south of the mesa late in the morning of the twenty-first, and Mortimore was wounded three times at McRae's battery. In fact, Hubbell's and Mortimore's companies had among the highest casualty rates of any on the field.[17]

Canby also attributed cowardice to Pino's regiment, suggesting that its failure to reinforce McRae's battery was one of the principal reasons for the loss of same. This situation, too, must be carefully evaluated. Pino's men were placed on the west bank, approximately eight hundred yards from (and out of sight of) the final location of the battery. Considering the time required for a courier to be dispatched and to cross the ford to Pino, for the 590-man regiment to form up and cross the river, and for the regiment to move to the battery through the riverside bosque, the fight would probably have been decided before they could have arrived in force. Estimates on the length of time from Green's order until the battery was largely overrun range from eight to fifteen minutes. Even under optimal conditions, with experienced troops, it would probably have taken Pino at least twenty to thirty minutes to form his companies into a column of fours, to ford three hundred yards of armpit-deep water with ammunition and weapons removed and held overhead to protect them from the water, to re-form on the opposite bank, and to engage the enemy. Thus, it seems unlikely that Pino's relatively inexperienced, and perhaps demoralized, troops could have had much of an impact on the outcome of the charge.[18]

Unquestionably, many of the men of the Second New Mexico Volunteers *were* reluctant to obey the order. After all, they could see their retreating comrades (both volunteer and regular), some of whom were undoubtedly wounded, and they could hear the sounds of battle and see the smoke and dust. Considering that these troops had never been in a major battle before, it does not seem surprising that they may have been a little slow to obey. However, one company and part of a second did cross and fight that afternoon. Beyond this, it must be noted that two of Pino's severest critics—Canby and Donaldson—were not direct observers of the volunteers' alleged reluctance to cross and fight. Both of these men were at or near the battery itself and so relied on the reports of others to assert that Pino's delay was due to cowardice rather than to simple inexperience and lack of training. In fact, Canby noted that Pino served with "zeal and energy."[19]

If the performance of the volunteers is to be scrutinized, so must the performance of some of the regulars. For example, Governor Connelly attributes some of the volunteers' lack of resolve to the refusal of the regulars next to them to advance.[20] Collins says that "the conduct of the two companies of *regulars* and volunteers was shamefully disgraceful and cowardly [emphasis added]" and Plympton, though blaming the situation on the "Mexicans," notes that their precipitous retreat to the river "took with them a portion of the left of my battalion."[21]

Lieutenant Colonel Roberts suggested that Duncan's conservatism in the morning destroyed an opportunity to seal the fate of the Texans at the lower ford. Canby suggests that Lord's inability to reinforce McRae was not totally acceptable (although it should be noted that a later court of inquiry exonerated Lord and that officer was later recognized for gallantry at the Battle of Gettysburg),[22] and Canby's operational control over the repositioning of McRae's battery and its supporting forces certainly must be questioned.

Despite the loss of the battle and questions about the performance of Lord, Plympton, and Duncan, Canby saw fit to give battlefield promotions (brevets) to eight of his officers, including one from the less-than-totally-successful Tenth Infantry, who was captured while crossing the river, and one of the two cavalry leaders who turned away from the battery. The former individual, Captain George Rossell, was said by some to be a "notorious coward" who had to have a guard mounted over his tent to prevent the men from harming him.[23] While some of these brevets were clearly well deserved (for example, those of Roberts and Wingate), a cynic looking at the overall picture might find this gesture to be rather self-serving.[24]

Terrain.

The Texans had ensconced themselves in the old riverbed behind the series of sand embankments. This allowed them to resist several Federal assaults and to redeploy their forces essentially without observation. In addition, Green was able to move his artillery and Lockridge's troops to his right and create a momentary local numerical and firepower advantage. They were able to achieve this advantage totally unbeknownst to the Union forces and were thus able to use the element of surprise to their considerable advantage.

Some "What Ifs"

Although the outcome of Valverde is well-known, it may be instructive to speculate about how things might have been different. In particular, four scenarios come to mind:

What if Canby had intercepted Green downriver from Fort Craig on or about February 12, before the bulk of the Confederate army had arrived, or on February 19, during the Paraje crossing?

What if Duncan had pursued Pyron and Raguet more aggressively in the morning before Scurry and Green had had a chance to bring the rest of the Confederate forces to the ford?

What if Canby had held McRae at his original position and allowed Duncan to continue to roll up the Texan's left wing following Raguet's charge?

What if Sibley had been successful at Valverde and Glorieta and had managed to carve out his "Western Confederacy"?

Scenario no. 1—An early attack.

The clear advantage of a Union attack on February 12 or 13 would have been that Sibley's forces were strung out along the road from Fort Thorn to just south of Fort Craig, whereas Canby could have massed between two thousand and three thousand troops. On the other hand, Canby's movements could not have been done covertly and his move downriver would have taken from one to two days. In that time, the Confederates might have been able to substantially shore up their position. That notwithstanding, Canby probably would have won such a fight, particularly since his numerical advantage would have been between 1.5:1 and 3:1. In addition, the Texans were somewhat debilitated because their train had lagged behind and they were short of food, ammunition, and blankets.

By February 19 the Confederate Brigade was fully formed and Canby would have had to take his New Mexico Volunteers into "harm's way" to reach the Texans. While the Texans would have been more vulnerable if they could have been intercepted crossing the river, it would have been impossible for Canby to have achieved much surprise and only a fraction of Sibley's force would have actually been in the water at any given time. Therefore, it seems unlikely that Canby would have gained much of an advantage in that fight.

Scenario no. 2—Duncan fights harder in the morning.

By 10:00 A.M., the Union forces had clear artillery supremacy plus a slight numerical advantage, although they didn't realize it because of the terrain and foliage near the lower ford. Had Duncan pursued his advantage per Roberts's entreaties and allowed Roberts to cross the batteries in the late morning instead of early afternoon, Roberts might well have been able to roll up the Texans' left before Green and the Fifth Regiment arrived. With the arrival of Selden and Green at noon, Roberts still enjoyed a slight numerical advantage as well as the firepower advantage afforded by the combination of Hall's and McRae's batteries over Teel's and Reily's lighter artillery. It seems unlikely that Pyron, Raguet, and Scurry could have withstood such an onslaught, particularly if the Federals had started a concentrated attack from an enfilading position near the mesa.

Scenario no. 3—Canby pivots on McRae's battery without
    advancing same.

Given the thirst of the Texans and the seemingly inexorable advance of Roberts on his left, Green's charge was probably inevitable, regardless of McRae's location. Had Canby left the battery where it was, the Confederates would have had to deal with an additional quarter-mile of canister and shell (four to eight additional rounds from each of the six guns). This distance would have given Canby several more minutes to recall Wingate and Carson from the right wing, to bring Claflin and Lord's cavalry to protect his right, to get Pino's reinforcements into the fray, and would have placed the battery in a less vulnerable position, much closer to the remainder of its original protective force.

All in all, this position probably would have made the difference: both Scurry and Raguet would have been repulsed; Duncan would have rolled up the Texas left; the men of the Third Cavalry would have attacked the Confederate train and Sibley's invasion would have been over.

Scenario no. 4—Sibley's dream comes true.

Given the Texans' logistics, the politics of the West at the time, and the Federal forces in the region, Sibley's dream was truly a long shot. However, the pot of gold at the end of his rainbow was a big one. Since Lincoln financed his war effort, in large part, from the gold fields of California and Colorado, a cutoff of those bullion supplies would have been disastrous for the Union and a hard-currency shot in the arm for Jefferson Davis's cash-poor Confederacy.

In addition, the Federal blockade would have had to expand to include parts of Mexico and California, a task that would have sorely challenged the Union navy in those days before the Panama Canal.

So Jefferson Davis had little to lose and much to gain. As for Canby, the battle was his to win or lose and he "chose" the latter. In retrospect, he and his officers have no one to blame but themselves.

After those frenetic days of early 1862, the ford at Valverde reverted once again to a quiet crossroads. The railroad came in 1880, cutting across the western part of the battlefield, and farmers from San Marcial and the villages of Valverde (and later Clyde) farmed the area north of the mesa until the flood of 1929 turned it into a marshy swamp. Today, with the creation of Elephant Butte reservoir, the tamarisk "invasion," and the construction of conveyance channels and irrigation canals by the Bureau of Reclamation, the battlefield itself is no more. The only record of the carnage of that cold February day in 1862 is a marker set up in 1936 at the San Marcial turn-off on old U.S. 85 by the United Daughters of the Confederacy to honor the Confederate officers and men who died in the battle.

Between seven thousand and ten thousand Civil War battles and skirmishes have been identified by various historians. In these engagements over 1,100,000 men were either killed or wounded.[25] On this scale, Valverde's 500 killed and wounded go almost unnoticed. Nonetheless, the Confederate invasion of New Mexico—a long shot with the potential of a huge pay-off—could have ended at Valverde. Had it ended there, the course of the Civil War would have been little changed. There might not have been a heroic Tom Green and his brigade to fight along the Red River, but others would surely have taken that role. There might not have been the need to make a hero out of John Chivington and so the abhorrent Sand Creek massacre could perhaps have been avoided, but there would certainly have been other atrocities against the Native Americans. The major effect of a Union victory at Valverde, particularly a morning victory, would have been the saving of the lives and limbs of about seven hundred brave men on both sides who were killed or wounded at McRae's battery, at Apache Canyon, at Glorieta, and at Peralta.

On the other hand, had Sibley's "impossible dream" come true, the course of the war would have been drastically altered, and U.S. history would certainly have been changed.

The Battle of Valverde was, in point of fact, the touchstone event of the Confederate invasion of New Mexico. Because of Valverde, Sibley's campaign was doomed and the outcome at Glorieta, though a fierce and bitter contest, was predestined. This said, the ultimate impact of Valverde is in the attitudes it fostered and the lives it cost—legacies that would survive long after the military significance of this nasty little fight had disappeared.

Appendix

Unit Strengths and Casualties at Valverde

Unit Strengths

In order to better understand the Battle of Valverde, it is important to understand the pre-battle unit strengths and the total casualties by organization. This appendix provides those data and describes the process used to arrive at the figures used in the text.

Confederate Unit Strengths

Hall provides a company-by-company analysis of the unit strengths based on an analysis of muster rolls, service records, and so forth.[1] The results shown below are based on the numbers that Hall cites as "effectives on the eve of the invasion," which I have taken to mean on or about February 7, 1862, when the army left Fort Thorn.

Regiment	Company	No.
Hdqtrs	n/a (Sibley)	17
Fourth	HQ (Scurry)	18
	A (Hardeman)	94
	B (Scarborough)	102
	C (Hampton)	80
	D (Leseur)	82
	E (Buckholts)	72
	F (Crosson)	72
	G (van den Heuvel)	71
	H (Alexander)	68
	I (Nunn)	86
	K (Foard)	70
	Arty (Reily)	35
	Total	850

Regiment	Company	No.
Fifth	HQ (Green)	13
	A (Shropshire)	98
	B (Lang)	70
	C (Shannon)	93
	D (Ragsdale)	73
	E (McPhaill)	88
	F (Campbell)	99
	G (McCown)	69
	H (Pridgen)	86
	I (Killough)	56
	K (Jordan)	61
	Arty (Wood)	27
	Total	833

Regiment	Company	No.
Seventh	HQ (Sutton)	18
	A (Jordan)	72
	B (Hoffmann)	84
	F (Wiggins)	86
	H (Adair)	84
	I (Gardner)	85
	Total	429
Baylor's (Second Rgt)	HQ (Pyron)	6
	B (Jett)	86
	D (Walker)	85
	E (Stafford)	79
	Arty (Teel)	89
	San Eliz (Nicholson)	51
	AZ Rngrs (Frazier)	56
	Brigands (Phillips)	13
	Total	465

Thus, the total Sibley Brigade was about 2,590 men. There are a few documented losses between leaving Fort Thorn and February 21 (for example, Private Kemp) and there surely must have been a few additional desertions, returns to Fort Thorn with messages, illness, and so on. However, I will use 2,590, distributed as noted herein, as my Confederate breakdown.

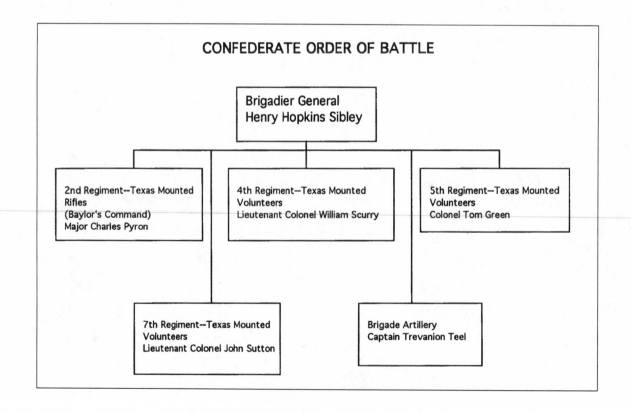

CONFEDERATE ORDER OF BATTLE

Brigadier General Henry Hopkins Sibley

2nd Regiment—Texas Mounted Rifles (Baylor's Command) Major Charles Pyron

4th Regiment—Texas Mounted Volunteers Lieutenant Colonel William Scurry

5th Regiment—Texas Mounted Volunteers Colonel Tom Green

7th Regiment—Texas Mounted Volunteers Lieutenant Colonel John Sutton

Brigade Artillery Captain Trevanion Teel

CONFEDERATE HEADQUARTERS

Brigadier General Henry H. Sibley

Major Alexander Jackson
Captain Willis Robards
Lieutenant Thomas Ochiltree
Lieutenant Joseph Dwyer
Major Samuel Magoffin
Dr. Edward Covey

PYRON'S BATTALION
SECOND REGIMENT--TEXAS MOUNTED RIFLES

Major Charles Pyron

Company B--
Lieutenant William Jett

Company D--
Captain James Walker

Company E--
Captain Ike Stafford

San Elizaro Spy Company--
Lieutenant Lemuel Nicholson

Arizona Rangers--
Captain George Frazier

Brigands--
Captain John Phillips

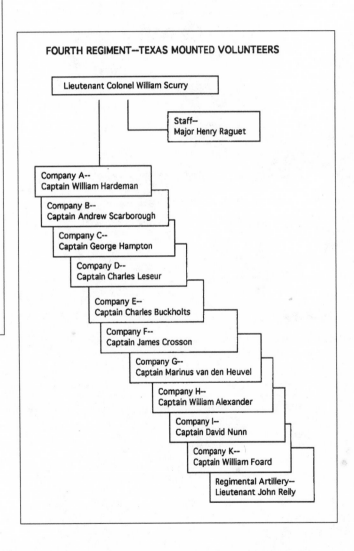

FOURTH REGIMENT--TEXAS MOUNTED VOLUNTEERS

Lieutenant Colonel William Scurry

Staff--
Major Henry Raguet

Company A--
Captain William Hardeman

Company B--
Captain Andrew Scarborough

Company C--
Captain George Hampton

Company D--
Captain Charles Leseur

Company E--
Captain Charles Buckholts

Company F--
Captain James Crosson

Company G--
Captain Marinus van den Heuvel

Company H--
Captain William Alexander

Company I--
Captain David Nunn

Company K--
Captain William Foard

Regimental Artillery--
Lieutenant John Reily

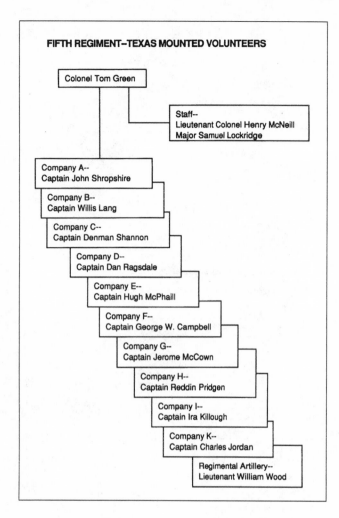

FIFTH REGIMENT--TEXAS MOUNTED VOLUNTEERS

Colonel Tom Green

Staff--
Lieutenant Colonel Henry McNeill
Major Samuel Lockridge

Company A--
Captain John Shropshire

Company B--
Captain Willis Lang

Company C--
Captain Denman Shannon

Company D--
Captain Dan Ragsdale

Company E--
Captain Hugh McPhaill

Company F--
Captain George W. Campbell

Company G--
Captain Jerome McCown

Company H--
Captain Reddin Pridgen

Company I--
Captain Ira Killough

Company K--
Captain Charles Jordan

Regimental Artillery--
Lieutenant William Wood

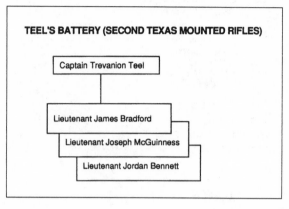

TEEL'S BATTERY (SECOND TEXAS MOUNTED RIFLES)

Captain Trevanion Teel

Lieutenant James Bradford

Lieutenant Joseph McGuinness

Lieutenant Jordan Bennett

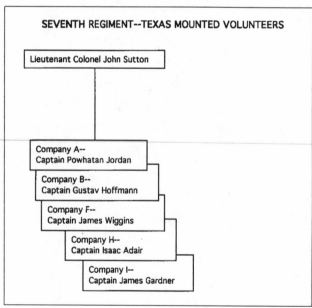

SEVENTH REGIMENT--TEXAS MOUNTED VOLUNTEERS

Lieutenant Colonel John Sutton

Company A--
Captain Powhatan Jordan

Company B--
Captain Gustav Hoffmann

Company F--
Captain James Wiggins

Company H--
Captain Isaac Adair

Company I--
Captain James Gardner

Union Unit Strengths

There are three main sources for Union unit strengths: the post returns from Fort Craig for late January and early February 1862, the report of Captain William Nicodemus on the columns for field operations,[2] and the collection of annotated, compiled service records collected by Charles Meketa and the author from the U.S. National Archives.[3] Some minor adjustments have been made as noted. Generally, these figures are company strengths and may not reflect detachments, AWOL, leave, and so forth between the date of the return and the battle. (It should be noted that, where possible, I have accounted for specified detachments such as the assignment of volunteers to the San Antonio grazing camp.) In addition, Canby says that "some detachments of regulars" were left at Fort Craig during the battle. Thus, as was the case with the Confederates, these should be considered maximum numbers for the Union battlefield strength at Valverde.

Regiment	Company	No.
HQ	n/a (Canby)	20
1st Cav	D (Lord)	66 [4]
	G (Claflin)	67
Third Cav (Duncan)	C (Howland) D (Treacy) G (Morris) K (Tilford)	210 [5]
Fifth Inf (Wingate)	B (Stone)	43 [6]
	D (Kopp)	67
	F (Cook)	76
	I (McDermott)	73
	K (Brotherton)	80
Seventh Inf (Selden)	C (Bascom)	82 [7]
	F (Rockwell)	69
	H (Ingraham)	82
Tenth Inf (Selden)	A (Rossell)	50
	F (Hall)	48 [8]
	H (Crossman?)	49
McRae	G/2C, I/3C	85 [9]
CO Vol.	(Dodd)	71 [10]
First NM (Carson)	Chavez	254
	Morrison	258
Second NM (Pino)	Chavez	295
	Pino	295 [11]
Third NM	Mortimore (A)	56
	B,C,E,G	334
	F,L (possibly attached to 2 NM)[12]	163
	H,K (at Fort Craig)	147 [13]
Fourth NM	Paul	65
Fifth NM (Roberts)	A (Barrientos)	63
	B (Hubbell)	71
Graydon		46 [14]
First NMM	Armijo	515 [15]
Second NMM	N. Pino	
	Total	3,801

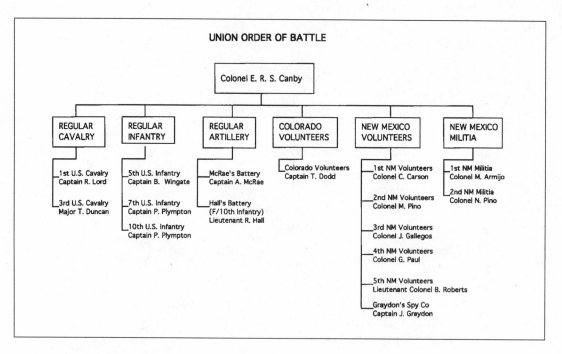

UNION ORDER OF BATTLE

Colonel E. R. S. Canby

REGULAR CAVALRY
- 1st U.S. Cavalry
  Captain R. Lord
- 3rd U.S. Cavalry
  Major T. Duncan

REGULAR INFANTRY
- 5th U.S. Infantry
  Captain B. Wingate
- 7th U.S. Infantry
  Captain P. Plympton
- 10th U.S. Infantry
  Captain P. Plympton

REGULAR ARTILLERY
- McRae's Battery
  Captain A. McRae
- Hall's Battery
  (F/10th Infantry)
  Lieutenant R. Hall

COLORADO VOLUNTEERS
- Colorado Volunteers
  Captain T. Dodd

NEW MEXICO VOLUNTEERS
- 1st NM Volunteers
  Colonel C. Carson
- 2nd NM Volunteers
  Colonel M. Pino
- 3rd NM Volunteers
  Colonel J. Gallegos
- 4th NM Volunteers
  Colonel G. Paul
- 5th NM Volunteers
  Lieutenant Colonel B. Roberts
- Graydon's Spy Co
  Captain J. Graydon

NEW MEXICO MILITIA
- 1st NM Militia
  Colonel M. Armijo
- 2nd NM Militia
  Colonel N. Pino

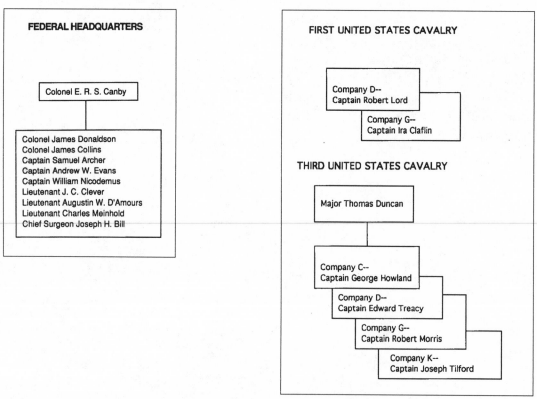

FEDERAL HEADQUARTERS

Colonel E. R. S. Canby

Colonel James Donaldson
Colonel James Collins
Captain Samuel Archer
Captain Andrew W. Evans
Captain William Nicodemus
Lieutenant J. C. Clever
Lieutenant Augustin W. D'Amours
Lieutenant Charles Meinhold
Chief Surgeon Joseph H. Bill

FIRST UNITED STATES CAVALRY

Company D--
Captain Robert Lord

Company G--
Captain Ira Claflin

THIRD UNITED STATES CAVALRY

Major Thomas Duncan

Company C--
Captain George Howland

Company D--
Captain Edward Treacy

Company G--
Captain Robert Morris

Company K--
Captain Joseph Tilford

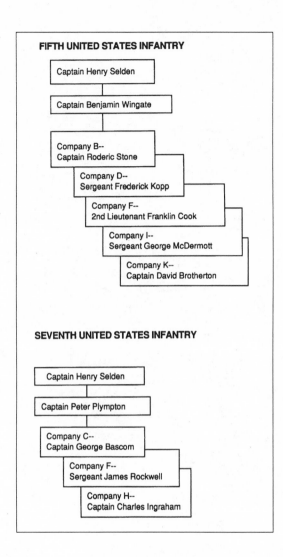

FIFTH UNITED STATES INFANTRY

Captain Henry Selden

Captain Benjamin Wingate

Company B--
Captain Roderic Stone

Company D--
Sergeant Frederick Kopp

Company F--
2nd Lieutenant Franklin Cook

Company I--
Sergeant George McDermott

Company K--
Captain David Brotherton

SEVENTH UNITED STATES INFANTRY

Captain Henry Selden

Captain Peter Plympton

Company C--
Captain George Bascom

Company F--
Sergeant James Rockwell

Company H--
Captain Charles Ingraham

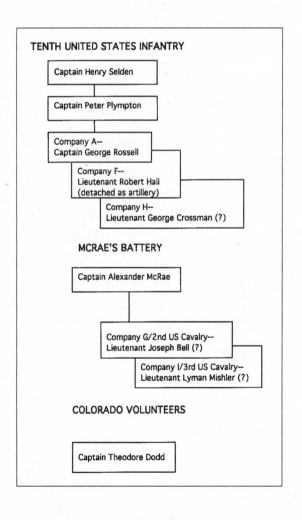

TENTH UNITED STATES INFANTRY

Captain Henry Selden

Captain Peter Plympton

Company A--
Captain George Rossell

Company F--
Lieutenant Robert Hall
(detached as artillery)

Company H--
Lieutenant George Crossman (?)

MCRAE'S BATTERY

Captain Alexander McRae

Company G/2nd US Cavalry--
Lieutenant Joseph Bell (?)

Company I/3rd US Cavalry--
Lieutenant Lyman Mishler (?)

COLORADO VOLUNTEERS

Captain Theodore Dodd

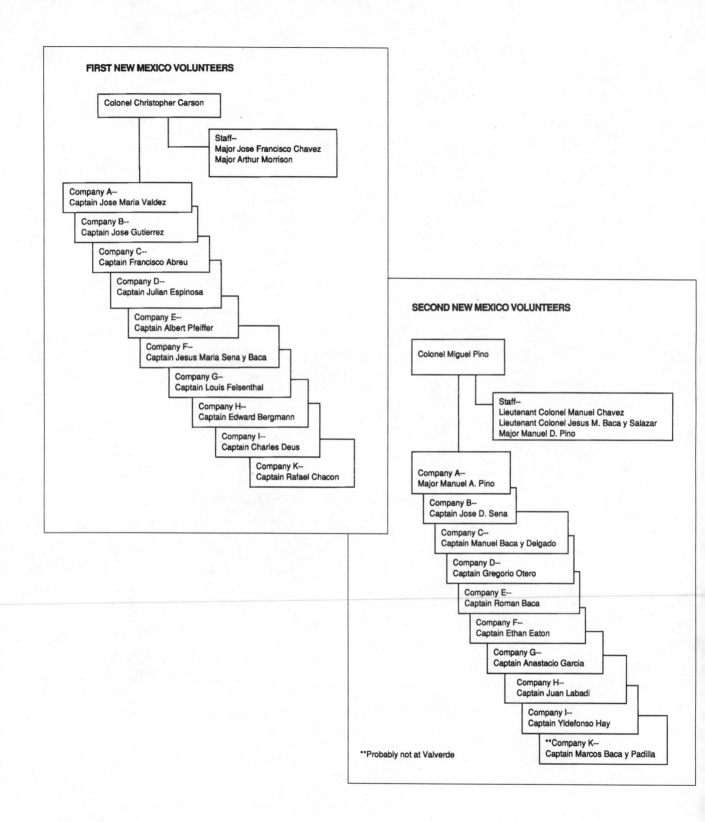

FIRST NEW MEXICO VOLUNTEERS

Colonel Christopher Carson

Staff--
Major Jose Francisco Chavez
Major Arthur Morrison

Company A--
Captain Jose Maria Valdez

Company B--
Captain Jose Gutierrez

Company C--
Captain Francisco Abreu

Company D--
Captain Julian Espinosa

Company E--
Captain Albert Pfeiffer

Company F--
Captain Jesus Maria Sena y Baca

Company G--
Captain Louis Felsenthal

Company H--
Captain Edward Bergmann

Company I--
Captain Charles Deus

Company K--
Captain Rafael Chacon

SECOND NEW MEXICO VOLUNTEERS

Colonel Miguel Pino

Staff--
Lieutenant Colonel Manuel Chavez
Lieutenant Colonel Jesus M. Baca y Salazar
Major Manuel D. Pino

Company A--
Major Manuel A. Pino

Company B--
Captain Jose D. Sena

Company C--
Captain Manuel Baca y Delgado

Company D--
Captain Gregorio Otero

Company E--
Captain Roman Baca

Company F--
Captain Ethan Eaton

Company G--
Captain Anastacio Garcia

Company H--
Captain Juan Labadi

Company I--
Captain Yldefonso Hay

**Company K--
Captain Marcos Baca y Padilla

**Probably not at Valverde

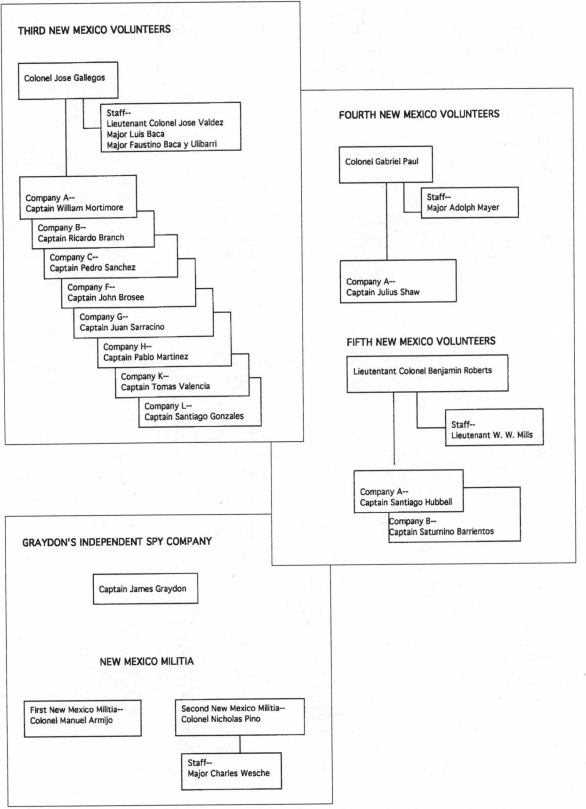

THIRD NEW MEXICO VOLUNTEERS

Colonel Jose Gallegos

Staff--
Lieutenant Colonel Jose Valdez
Major Luis Baca
Major Faustino Baca y Ulibarri

Company A--
Captain William Mortimore

Company B--
Captain Ricardo Branch

Company C--
Captain Pedro Sanchez

Company F--
Captain John Brosee

Company G--
Captain Juan Sarracino

Company H--
Captain Pablo Martinez

Company K--
Captain Tomas Valencia

Company L--
Captain Santiago Gonzales

FOURTH NEW MEXICO VOLUNTEERS

Colonel Gabriel Paul

Staff--
Major Adolph Mayer

Company A--
Captain Julius Shaw

FIFTH NEW MEXICO VOLUNTEERS

Lieutentant Colonel Benjamin Roberts

Staff--
Lieutenant W. W. Mills

Company A--
Captain Santiago Hubbell

Company B--
Captain Saturnino Barrientos

GRAYDON'S INDEPENDENT SPY COMPANY

Captain James Graydon

NEW MEXICO MILITIA

First New Mexico Militia--
Colonel Manuel Armijo

Second New Mexico Militia--
Colonel Nicholas Pino

Staff--
Major Charles Wesche

I have chosen to use the numbers listed above as the basis for the discussion in the text.

Casualties

I have used the conventional definition of a casualty as any man who is either killed, wounded, or missing. Howell says that twenty-one Union prisoners were captured[16]—these men are included in the missing total since they were subsequently unavailable for some period of time to the side that lost them. Mortally wounded men are included in the "killed" category.

Confederate Casualties

This specification of casualties is drawn from the muster roles in Hall's *Confederate Army of New Mexico* and the article by Thomas Ochiltree in the May 3, 1862, edition of the *San Antonio Herald*. In some cases, the Theophilus Noel diary also lists casualties, some of whom are not mentioned in the Confederate army list. These, too, are included and annotated as to source (Noel as such and the *San Antonio Herald* as SAH). Although Green shows one missing soldier (from Baylor's command), the detailed lists do not show any. Thus, I assume that the man whom Green found as missing immediately after the fight turned up as wounded or killed during later tallies. The only Confederate participant confirmed as missing was the wagonmaster from the Fourth Texas, mentioned by Peticolas.[17] In general, I defer to Hall's lists where conflicts arise, since he made a detailed survey of the actual service records of the soldiers. Although some have suggested that the Ochiltree article is a better source, Ochiltree himself suggests that there is some uncertainty in the numbers he is reporting.

Army Headquarters and Staff

wounded:
Willis Robards (wounded in lancer charge with Company B of the Fifth)

Fourth Regiment

Headquarters and Staff

killed:
Jere Odell

wounded:
Henry Raguet

missing:
unnamed wagonmaster

Company A

wounded:
Norval Cartwright
John Cook
William Fergerson
Joseph Francis
William Hardeman
Ralph Hunter
Benjamin Hysaw
Jesse Lott
Henry Maney
Robert McWright
Joseph Roberts
George White
Daniel L. Wiley

Company B

killed:
Arthur Brooks
Thomas Nixon
Jacob Talley (Noel)

wounded:
Joseph Bunton
Thompson Harris
Mat Hendricks
Jonathan Nix
James Stroud
Jeremiah Williams

Company C

wounded:
Louis Berkowitz
J. Crook (SAH)
Alfred Field
Otto Kleberg
George Hampton
William Mobley
William Onderdonk
S. Schmidt

Company D

killed:
Daniel Gilleland
Sims Slaughter

wounded:
Alexander Huffman
Peter Kolb

Company E

killed:
A. J. Long
T. J. Leatherman

wounded:
Y. Granthan

Company F

killed:
S. Dunham (Noel)
David McCormick

wounded:
John Cook
Napoleon Dial
James Gill
William Matthews

Company G

killed:
Henry Gaethe
Marinus van den Heuvel

wounded:
William Becker
Charles Korff
William Korff
Ernest Melchior
Charles Rhodius
Richard Schlick
Henry Spies
Joseph Stahmer
Julius Sternenberg
Hermann Trenckmann
John Voelkel

Company H

killed:
Moses Russell
Elisha Tindall
J. Walton
James Williams

wounded:
Napoleon Coats
James Castles
William Hardwick
Thomas Pitts
Hardy White

Company I

killed:
Zebadee Gossett

wounded:
R. Atmar
J. Atmar
A. Dawson
J. Sharp (SAH)
J. Stephenson

Company K

killed:
John Rodes
J. Vining

wounded:
John Campbell

Artillery
no casualties reported

Fifth Regiment

Headquarters and Staff

killed:
Samuel Lockridge

wounded:
Thomas Green

Company A

killed:
John David
David Hubbard
Martin Pankey
Sandford Putnam
Josiah Smith
J. Stolts

wounded:
Augustus Baker
F. Caldwell
John Campbell
Robert Carter
Peter Clapp
Suffield Clapp
William Davidson
Holman Donald
Thomas Gillespie
A. Grow
Samuel Henderson
John Knowles
Manly Knowlton
H. MacDonald (Noel)
George Martin
James McLeary
Robert Mitchell
John Montgomery
G. Roberts
August Schubert
George Sloneker

Company B

killed:
Demetrius Bass
William A. Bell
Francis Canty
Joseph Curry
John Daugherty
John Ferguson
Silas Ivans
Willis Lang
Isaac Marlin
Robert Mitchell
Henry Persons
Hilary Pierson

wounded:
Wade Coleman
Andrew Davis
James Forbes
Thomas Lea
John Parker
George Polster
Edmond Shelton
John Sowders

Company C

killed:
Silas Johnson

wounded:
Titus Johnson
J. Moore

Company D

killed:
William Tyson
Samuel Yokum

wounded:
David Brown
James Ladd
John Lorenz

Company E

killed:
James Boykin
Ross Myrick
Lewis Rosenberg

wounded:
W. Slade
John Tyson
John Wilkins
William Wilkins

Company F

killed:
William Craig
C. Lewis (Noel)
Charles Tidwell

wounded:
W. Anderson
C. Hensley
Gideon Keesee
D. Kothour
F. McMinn
Benton Seat

Company G

killed:
Henry Figley
Allen Jones

wounded:
John Byrnes
Jerry Perrine
A. Snow
Hugh Wiester

Company H

killed:
Harvey McClinton
Lucius Smith
Hosea Walling

wounded:
Fuller Ainsworth
Cornelius Bird
William Good
George Grooms

Simon Hager
Thomas Land
William Norman
Thomas Orenbaun

Company I

killed:
Henry Smith
Jared Winburn

wounded:
Luke Harrison

Company K

killed:
James Littlepage
Benton Martin
W. Shirley

wounded:
Jonathan Hogsett
Henry Sisk

Artillery
no casualties reported

Seventh Regiment

Headquarters and Staff

killed:
John Sutton

Company A
no casualties reported

Company B

killed:
Charles Nitsche

wounded:
Adolf Gelven
Charles Gordon (SAH)
Fred Harms
P. Linnartz
Peter Linnartz
A. Magnus
Henry McGrew (SAH)

Company F

killed:
Bruce Bradshaw
Thomas Garrison
A. Prather
Benjamin Richey

wounded:
T. Crews
L. Dial
Frank Elkins
James Grey
James Harris
H. Johnson
William Jones
J. Kendrick
Stephen Montgomery
J. Pruitt
B. Quaid
D. Sharp
William Wiggins

Company H
no casualties reported

Company I

killed:
Robert Cone
Jaspar Jones

wounded:
J. H. Alexander
John Barnett
James Gardner
Perry Holliman
Thomas Kennedy
Joseph Lyles
J. B. Tucker
A. Vannoy

Baylor's Command

Headquarters and Staff
no casualties reported

Company B
no casualties reported

Company D

killed:
Ed. Campion

wounded:
John Cleghorn
Note: SAH says four additional
    unnamed men were
    wounded.

Company E
no casualties reported

Teel's Battery

killed:
Herman Lowenstein
Joseph Page
Atticus Ryan (detached from
    Company B)

wounded:
James Logan
John Maloney
Nicholas Mitchell
Trevanion Teel

San Elizaro Spies

killed:
SAH says two unnamed men
    were killed.

wounded:
Silas Merchant

Arizona Rangers

wounded:
SAH says one unnamed man
    was slightly wounded.

Brigands
no casualties reported

Summary of Confederate Casualties

	Killed	Wounded	%		Killed	Wounded	%
Headquarters		1	6	*Seventh Regiment*	8	28	8
				HQ	1	0	6
Fourth Regiment	20	57	9	A	0	0	
HQ*	1	1	11	B	1	7	10
A	0	13	14	F	4	13	20
B	3	6	9	H	0	0	
C	0	8	10	I	2	8	12
D	2	2	5				
E	2	1	4				
F	2	4	8	*Baylor's*	6	11	4
G	2	11	18				
H	4	5	13	HQ	0	0	
I	1	5	7				
K	2	1	4	B	0	0	
Arty	0	0					
				D	1	5	7
Fifth Regiment	38	60	12				
HQ	1	1	15	E	0	0	
A	6	21	28				
B	12	8	29	Arty	3	4	8
C	1	2	3				
D	2	3	7	San Elizaro	2	1	6
E	3	4	8				
F	3	6	9	AZ Rangers	0	1	2
G	2	4	9				
H	3	8	13	Brigands	0	0	
I	2	1	5				
K	3	2	8	Total	71	157	9**
Arty	0	0					
				Grand Total	229*		

*Missing = 1: the unnamed wagonmaster of the Fourth Regiment was captured on the morning of the twenty-first. He is the only missing Texan.

**Less the three hundred or so men who remained with the train, this casualty percentage per man engaged becomes about 10 percent.

Union Casualties

There are several sources for this compilation of Union casualties: the post-battle post return from Fort Craig; a list dated February 1862; a list of Union dead from Valverde that was compiled and placed into a time capsule in the Civil War memorial in Santa Fe in 1867; a list of dead from all units dated March 14, 1867; a list of casualties from the Colorado Volunteers; the diary entries of Alonzo Ickis; an article in the Santa Fe *Gazette* dated May 10, 1862; and service record entries for the New Mexico Volunteers and Colorado Volunteers, which have been reviewed and/or compiled by Charles Meketa and the author. Not all of the lists are consistent, but I have assumed that if an individual is listed as a casualty on two or more lists (or on his service record), he was confirmed to be so. I have indicated with question marks those men who only appear on a single list. Note that all of the uncertainties are for regular army. I have been unable to locate compiled service records for any regular army units that participated in the Battle of Valverde.

Two further notes are needed. First, I have not included the three casualties from preparatory fights (Hugh Brown of the Colorado Volunteers who was killed on the twentieth, Private Benjamin Baum of the Third New Mexico, who died on the nineteenth from wounds suffered on the sixteenth, and Private John Mesner of the First New Mexico Volunteers, who was wounded on the twentieth (note that Private Mesner recovered and fought on the twenty-first when he was wounded again—an occurrence that is included in the total). In addition, I have included McRae and Mishler with McRae's battery rather than their respective assigned regular army units. I have also included Bascom with the Seventh U.S. Infantry rather than his assigned unit (Sixteenth U.S. Infantry).

Fifth Infantry, First Column (Wingate)

Company B

killed:
Nicholas Hays
John Pollock
Luther Shepherd
Roderic Stone

wounded:
Patrick Ryan

Company D

killed:
John Ford
Andres Kinberger
Patrick Hughes
John Murphy
John Stewart
Henry Schlutter
Benjamin Wingate

wounded:
James Broadbent
Frederick Bently
William Harkness
Dennis Lipencott
Thomas Murray
Michael O'Hara
John Salkauld
Joseph Wells

missing:
Timothy Quinn

Company F

killed:
Joseph Hudson
Jacob Levy
Simon Rothschilds

wounded:
Francis Bellien (?)
Cornelius Cary
Patrick Coleman
Phalen Cromer (?)

Michael Green
John Kennedy
Thomas MacDonald
James McGuire
Thomas Quigley (?)
Patrick Simons
Patrick Smith
James Snyder
Dennis Sullivan

Company I

wounded:
John Cass
Joseph Hoag
George McDermott
John Morris
Henry Sawton

Fifth Infantry, Second Column

Company K

killed:
Thomas Leavy
William Lumberg (?)

wounded:
John Buchanan
Thomas Dalton
Thomas Fraley

Seventh Infantry, Companies C and F (Plympton)

Company C

killed:
George Bascom
John Fitzgerald
John Leibrich
James McDonald
Timothy Sullivan
James Williden

wounded:
James Cavinder
Patrick Carroll
Thomas Dowary

Daniel Harrington
William Hatton
Michael Mara
Robert Simpson
William Smith

Company F

killed:
Thomas Arnold
Thomas Carey
John Douglas
John Ellard
Joseph Falgan
Eugene Gibbons
Alexander Gillon
William James
L. Johns II
Emile Kahn
Peter McCae
John Murray
James Nolan
Curran O'Brien
James O'Brien
Owen O'Connell
James Reilly
James Rockwell
John Rumbell
Philip Shoemaker
Michael Smith
Patrick Smith
John Tehan

wounded:
Robert Adair
Benjamin Baker
Charles Ballinder
Edward Bohe
Charles Brady
John Brown
John Crangle
Michael Dillon
Julius Dollars
Charles East
Theodore Falke
John Foley
Henry Hay

Joseph Kelly
William Ladery (?)
John Marks
Patrick McKenna
Patrick O'Brien
William Rethney
Andrew Seamans
William Smith
Louis Ulrich
Charles Williamson

missing:
John Conway (?)
George Putman
Daniel McCany

**Seventh Infantry, Company H
(Ingraham)**

wounded:
William Ward

**Tenth Infantry, First Column
(Plympton)**

Company A

killed:
Peter Collins
John Haggart
Samuel Miller
John Riechling
William Scheer
Charles Washburn

wounded:
Oliver Barney
Joseph Brant
W. H. Conroy
Andrew Falry
Leander Harrison

missing:
John Dillon
John Kane
William Montgomery
Charles Murphy
George Rossell
D. S. Skinner

Company H

killed:
John Brown
Carl Christianson
Thomas Crotty
Mathew Harrison
Thomas Kelly
John Schweer

wounded:
James Drake
Timothy Flynn
Lorenzo Gress
William Haydock
Augustus Kensch
John Laddy
John Loughlan
Timothy Hoffman (?)
Joseph Sesmore
Robert Sullivan

**Tenth Infantry, Company F
(Hall's Battery)**

no casualties reported

McRae's Battery

killed:
Emil Bride
Michael Brown (?)
Simon Cooke
James Courtney
John Driscoll
Joseph Eckels
M. L. Hoyd
Thomas Hughes
John Knox
John Ludwig
James Martin
Alexander McRae
Joseph McTeague
Lyman Mishler
Patrick Murray
Michael O'Brien
John Phillips

Patrick Scanlan
John Westervitt

wounded:
Barney Dugan
Jacob Eggerstedt
Otto Eggenschwaller
William Foster
Edward Higgins (?)
Thomas Hilman (?)
Kearns (?)
Mespers (?)
Mathew Meyer
Otto Maine
Richard Morrison
John Orr
Thomas Quigley
Daniel Riley
William Salkland (?)
William Shallard
Robert Sitzsinger
Samuel Smith
William C. Smith
William H. Smith
Edwin Sullivan
John Sullivan
Richard Thompson (?)
Rudolph Wolfer

missing:
Terence Brady
John McCarthy

Third Cavalry

wounded:
Peter Allworm
Sylvester Bennett
William Berny
Frederick Buhler
Frederick Fellman
James Jackson
Daniel Johnson
Michael Kennedy
James McNally
G. W. Merrymas

First Cavalry

Company D (Lord)

killed:
William Monroe

wounded:
James Dunn
Nathan Golliher

missing:
Charles Taylor

Company G (Claflin)
no casualties reported

Colorado Volunteers[18]

killed:
John McKee
Nelson West
Harrison Woodward

wounded:
Thomas Anderson
William Anderson
John Branch
Frederick Bridgement
Joachim Burts
William Cook
James Custer
Abram Deman
Patrick Duffy
Andrew R. Duran
Francis Finch
Samuel Hay
William F. Kenton
Franz Pampanch
Thomas Payne
Samuel Pickler
Ludlow Pruden
James Robinson
Alborn Sandborn
Edwin Sanford
George Simpson
Asa Talbot
Joseph Thomas

John Thompson
Andrew Thompson
Seymour Vaughan
John M. Weaver
George Williams
John Young

missing, prisoners:
John W. Ames
Sylvester Gilson
Andrew Grover
James Martin
Sydenham Mills
Samuel Westerfield
William Withington

missing (presumed deserter):
Harrison Berry

First New Mexico Volunteers

killed:
Marcelino Baca
Juan Cristobel Lucero (missing, assumed killed)

wounded:
Albino Brito
John Mesner

missing (and subsequently declared deserters):
Toribio Archuleta
Benito Atencio
Francisco Bustamante
Domingo Chavez
Rafael Jaques
Cornelio Jaramillo
Ignacio Martin
Salvador Martin
Melquades Montano
Francisco Ocana
Felipe Vasquez (subsequently tried and shot)
Manuel Vigil

Second New Mexico Volunteers

killed:
José Romero (Company C)
Antonio Valencia (Company F)

wounded:
Rafael Gallegos (Company C)
Teodicio Sabedra (Company I)

missing:
Based on service records, as many as 131 men may have deserted from the field.[19]

Third New Mexico Volunteers

Company A (Mortimore)

killed:
Thomas Gallagher
Alvino Herrera
Juan José Sanchez
Antonio Vasques

wounded:
José Crespin
Felipe Maes
William Mortimore
Edward Walters

missing; prisoner:
George Baker (Graydon's company attached to Mortimore)

missing, declared deserters, pardoned under GO43:
Cresenio Baca
Perfecto Baca
Juan Benevides
Leandro Benevides
Antonia Herrera
Jesús Legra
José Lobato
Miguel Lopez
Tranquilina Lopez
Fernando Maes

Marcus Medrano
Santiago Moya
Juan de Dios Pacheco
Julian Probencio
Carmel Romero
Joaquin Royval
Antonio Tapia
Ignacio Trujillo

Company B

killed:
Joaquin Suazo

missing, declared deserters:
Juan Cardenas (shown as Co A)
Gregorio Gallegos

Company C
no casualties reported

Company E
no casualties reported

Company F

killed:
José Martin

Company G

killed:
Rafael Sais

missing; declared deserters:
Jesús Gallegos
José Dolores Garcia

Company H

missing; declared deserters:
Trinidad Bachicha
Juan de Jesús Chaves
Rafael Lujan

Company K

missing; declared deserters:
José Martin
Espitacio Vigil
Juan Vigil

Company L

missing; declared deserter:
Juan de Jesús Lucero

Fourth New Mexico Volunteers

no casualties reported

Fifth New Mexico Volunteers

Company A (Hubbell)

killed:
José Clemente Alaria
Charles Benzinger
Pablo Candelario
Ramón Candelario
Juan Chaves (?)
Mariano Chaves
Marcelino Duran
Juan Garcia
Macani Garcia
Basilio Gonzales
Rumaldo Griego
Guadalupe Lopes
Diego Lucero
José Lucero
Juan Mexicanna
Pedro Padillo
Gomesindo Rivera
Benino Sanches
José Tapio
Pablo Zuni

wounded:
Rubio Cruz (?)
Basilio Martin
Antonio Montoya
Juan Pais
Ramón Rival
Clemente Sanches
José Sanches
Manual Trujillo
Felipe Turriete

*missing; no record of
desertion:*
Ramón Alaria
Ygnacio Sandoval

missing; declared deserters:
Espamino Chavez
Mauricio Chavez
José Garviso
José Guerrera
Jesús Marcus
Victoriano Montoya
José Peralto
Salvador Rial

Company B (Barrientos)

wounded:
Lorenzo Romero

Graydon's Spy Company
no casualties reported

First New Mexico Militia

no casualties reported

Second New Mexico Militia

no casualties reported

Total Union Casualties

	Killed	Wounded	Missing	%		Killed	Wounded	Missing	%
Federal Left					Tenth Infantry				
Headquarters/					(Hall)	0	0	0	
Staff	0	0	0		First Cavalry, Co. G				
Fifth Infantry					(Claflin)	0	0	0	
(Wingate)	14	27	1	16	Third Cavalry	0	10	0	5
B	4	1	0	12	First NM	2	2	12	3
D	7	8	1	24	Second NM	2	2	131	26
F	3	13	0	21	Third NM				
I	0	5	0	7	(Valdez)	3	0	5	
Seventh Infantry					Company B	1	0	2	
(Plympton)	29	31	3	42	Company C	0	0	0	
C	6	8	0	17	Company E	0	0	0	
F	23	23	3	71	Company F	1	0	0	
Tenth Infantry					Company G	1	0	1	
(Plympton)	12	15	6	33	Company L	0	0	1	
A	6	5	6	34	Fifth New Mexico, Co. A				
H	6	10	0	33	(Barrientos)	0	1	0	2
McRae's					Graydon	0	0	0	
Battery	19	24	2	53					
Colorado					**At Fort Craig**				
Volunteers	3	29	8	56	Third New Mexico	0	0	6	4
First Cavalry, Co. D					Company H	0	0	3	4
(Lord)	1	2	1	6	Company K	0	0	3	4
Third NM, Company A					Fourth New				
(Mortimore)	4	4	19	48	Mexico	0	0	0	
Fifth NM, Company B					First New Mexico				
(Hubbell)	20	9	10	55	Militia	0	0	0	
					Second New Mexico				
Federal Right					Militia	0	0	0	
Fifth Infantry, K									
(Brotherton)	2	3	0	6					
Seventh Infantry					Total	111	160	204	12**
(Ingraham)	0	1	0	1	Grand Total = 475				

**Excluding the men who remained to garrison the fort, this casualty percentage per man engaged becomes 17 percent. The percentage of killed and wounded per man engaged is 10 percent.

A Qualitative Evaluation of Union Casualties

Casualties were a significant measure of a unit's ability to fight again on the next day. Hence, men not present for muster were considered losses, regardless of the reason. In general, killed and wounded are not controversial—men generally found their way either to the morgue or the hospital, or they did not. The category "missing," however, introduces some complications.

Men who were "missing" could be dead but not found or identified, captured by the enemy, separated from their units by virtue of enemy action, or absent by virtue of desertion from the field. The challenge of accounting for the Union missing at Valverde was complicated by the peculiar circumstances of Canby's organization at Fort Craig and by the course of the battle itself.

Canby's thirty-eight-hundred-man force was truly a hodgepodge organization. Within the force there were fifteen identifiable, unrelated regiments or independent companies, including four totally separate jurisdictional groups (regular army—infantry, cavalry, and artillery, New Mexico Volunteers, New Mexico Militia, and Colorado Volunteers). Many of these organizations were not only new to Fort Craig, but also new to the military lifestyle. Most of the New Mexicans (both officers and enlisted men) spoke and wrote English only sparingly, if at all.

The chaotic, early evening culmination of the battle for McRae's battery also enhanced the confusion with regard to accounting for personnel. As the Texans overran the battery, units were separated and prisoners were taken. As the Union troops (both regulars and volunteers) fled across the river, some were shot, some no doubt were swept away and drowned, and some made it across the river and simply ran away. Since the Texans controlled the field, any Federals who ran north would have had to slip through the Confederate lines to return to Fort Craig immediately, and they may well have elected to "lie low" until Sibley and his men left the area.

Prisoners were another issue. Neither side really wanted to be bothered with the care and feeding of enemy soldiers. This was particularly true for the Texans, who were traveling light and were already short of supplies. Therefore, men who were captured or who surrendered were generally disarmed, threatened with grievous bodily harm if they should be caught fighting again, and released (sometimes referred to as "being paroled") within a few days.

Therefore, in evaluating the significance of the casualties specified in this appendix, one must consider several factors. Initially, the question of availability to fight a follow-up battle on the twenty-second must have been high on Canby's list of concerns, so he would have looked at the total "unavailability" as an important metric. Secondly, the impact on morale of missing men was almost worse than those who were confirmed to be dead or wounded. Where were your friends? Were they lying somewhere slowly bleeding to death? Had they run off? The uncertainty must have significantly demoralized units with large number of unaccounted-for men, at least in the immediate aftermath of the fight. Furthermore, the commanders must have been concerned that their losses were, perhaps, the enemy's gains—had the men merely deserted, or had they joined the Texans?

Finally, what was the long-term impact? Over a period of several days, most of the men who had become separated or had been captured were "repatriated" or confirmed to be dead or wounded. For example, Ickis notes only one man from the Colorado Volunteers, Harrison Berry, as AWOL and names seven prisoners. The other eleven Coloradans who are listed as missing in the initial post-battle report were eventually determined to be either killed or wounded. Based on post-battle reports and subsequent post returns this seems to be true for all but perhaps two of the thirty regulars initially identified as missing by Canby.

As to the New Mexico Volunteers, the picture is further clouded by the animosity and lack of trust between the regular officers, especially Colonel Canby, and the volunteers. As blame was passed out in the aftermath of the defeat, Canby and his officers pointed the finger at the New Mexico Volunteers. Thus, many of the entries on service records indicate that the men were declared to be deserters shortly after turning up missing at the battle. However, many of these same "deserters" were subsequently reenlisted *without prejudice* only a few months later, when the New Mexico Cavalry was formed. In addition, many of the "missing" men were discharged en masse on May 7 under General Amnesty Order no. 43,[20] which pardoned all deserters

from the volunteers and militia. By September of 1862, 852 men had returned to their homes under this amnesty.[21] Although some of these discharges were annotated "without honor," perhaps signifying a true deserter, many were simply discharged with no explanatory notes.

The Second New Mexico Volunteers are something of a special case in this regard. Service records indicate that 129 of the 523 men were declared to be deserters, and 77 of these men received amnesty under General Order 43. This particular regiment had been involved in the unpleasantness in Belen in January and probably were more mutinous and/or demoralized than the other volunteer regiments. However, given the general confusion near the end of the battle and Canby's apparent desire to release that portion of his force which he perceived to be more of a burden than a help, the potential for a misunderstanding of orders to retreat or to regroup is high. It is worth noting that Pino makes no mention of mass desertions in his official report of the battle and Canby does not question that report. In addition, Canby's after-action report dated March 1, 1862, shows zero missing from the Second New Mexico. This discrepancy between the service record entries of desertions on February 21 and the battle report is so striking as to suggest that the 131 number may be a politically motivated late addition.

Thus, I conclude that many of the missing New Mexico Volunteers probably returned to their units within a short period of time and simply became historical victims of poor record keeping or political expediency.

Notes

The material in this book has been drawn from a large number of sources, not all of which are in full agreement concerning the events that transpired in New Mexico in February 1862. The text is my best effort in resolving source discrepancies in terms of units involved, times of engagements, outcomes, and so forth. The notes for each section provide justification for my choice of scenarios as well as documenting "dissenting" viewpoints.

Three principal types of sources have been used for this work: firsthand accounts, third-person accounts, and overviews. The firsthand accounts can be further subdivided into those written at the time of the battle or shortly thereafter (for example, the Peticolas diary and

many of the Official Reports) and those written later (such as the Chacón and Bell accounts). Where possible, I have based my description on the real-time, firsthand reports. In those situations where such reports are silent or at variance, I have attempted to resolve the discrepancies using the recollections. Finally, I have used the other sources to expand upon the participant's accounts, to enrich the account, and to attempt to further resolve discrepancies.

The following abbreviations appear in the notes:
OR—*Official Reports of the War of the Rebellion*
NA—National Archives of the United States
RG—Microfilm Record Group from the U.S. National Archives

Chapter 1

1. Historians estimate that over fifty thousand books, more than one per day, have been written about the Civil War since it ended at Appomattox in April 1865. From my perspective, the best overviews are Shelby Foote's trilogy *The Civil War: A Narrative* (New York: Vintage Books, 1986), and Henry Woodhead's twenty-two-volume Time-Life Civil War series, *The Civil War* (Alexandria: Time-Life Books, 1985). In my opinion, the best overviews of the war in New Mexico are Hall's *Sibley's New Mexico Campaign* (Austin: University of Texas

Press, 1960), and Josephy's *The Civil War in the American West* (New York: Alfred A. Knopf, 1991).

2. The westernmost engagement of the Civil War is usually said to have occurred near Picacho Peak, north of Tucson, Arizona, on April 15, 1862 (Josephy, *Civil War in the American West*, p. 90). However, Fireman suggests that incidents may have occurred as far west as the Colorado River and Long notes incidents in San Francisco Bay and a naval engagement even farther west in the Straits of

Shimonoseki near Yokohama, Japan. Bert M. Fireman, "How Far Westward the Civil War," in Robert B. Cormack, ed., *The 1963 All Posse Corral Brand Book of the Denver Posse of the Westerners* (Morrison: Buffalo Bill Press, 1965), pp. 164–70; E. B. Long, "War Beyond the River—Our Civil War and the Uncivil West," in Alan J. Stewart, ed., *The Denver Westerners Brand Book* (Boulder: Johnson Publishing Co., 1977), pp. 92–118.

3. New Mexico had a two-hundred-year tradition of Indian slavery and a system of indentured servitude called peonage, which was felt by many to be more cruel than Negro slavery in the South. For example, although peons could not be bought or sold, landlords or overseers were under no obligation to retain or to care for peons who were aged, infirm, or otherwise unable to work. Loomis M. Ganaway, *New Mexico and the Sectional Controversy* (Albuquerque: University of New Mexico Press, 1944), pp. 9–13. The 1860 census listed eighty-five "free coloreds" as the only blacks in the territory.

4. Trevanion T. Teel, "Sibley's New Mexico Campaign: Its Objects and the Causes of Its Failure," in Robert Underwood Johnson and Clarence Clough Buel, eds., *Battles and Leaders of the Civil War*, vol. 2 (1887, repr., Secaucus: Castle Press, n.d.) p. 700.

5. Don Alberts, "The Corps of Engineers and New Mexico's Water," *New Mexico Historical Review* 51 (April 1976), pp. 93–108.

6. T. W. Robinson, "Introduction, Spread and Areal Extent of Saltcedar in the Western States" (United States Geological Survey Professional Paper 491A, 1965) pp. A5–A7.

7. Mesa del Contadero (also known as Black Mesa) was a well-known geographical marker at the north end of the desert crossing known as Jornada del Muerto (Journey of the Dead Man). It was probably named for the narrow defile on its western edge, where the river passes through a gorge between the mesa and the western highlands. This gorge served to impound, rest, and count livestock prior to the strenuous passage across the Jornada. Michael P. Marshall and Henry J. Walt, *Rio Abajo—Prehistory and History of a Rio Grande Province* (Santa Fe: New Mexico Office of Historic Preservation, 1984), p. 240, and Spencer Wilson, "El Contadero," *Rio Grande History* 6 (1976), pp. 6–7.

Chapter 2

1. In his treatise on the history of the Rio Grande, Paul Horgan notes that Valverde was used as a meeting place and way station by military expeditions, traders, and others. Paul Horgan, *Great River* (New York: Rinehart and Company, 1954). Marshall and Walt echo this description (Marshal and Walt, *Rio Abajo*, pp. 286–87).

2. Marshall and Walt, *Rio Abajo*, p. 286.

3. Ibid., *Rio Abajo*, p. 287. The February 1862 post return for Fort Craig notes 128 civilian employees including teamsters, blacksmiths, and spies. Some of these men no doubt lived in or near the village of Valverde, and a significant fraction of the 4,045 dollars paid to the civilian workers that month may have found its way into the Valverde "economy" (Returns from U.S. Military Posts, RG 94, M617, NA).

4. The definitive biography of Henry Sibley is Jerry Thompson's *Henry Hopkins Sibley, Confederate General of the West* (Natchitoches: Northwestern State University Press, 1987).

5. Marc Simmons, *Albuquerque* (Albuquerque: University of New Mexico Press, 1982), p. 176.

6. "Brevet" ranks were honorary advancements given to officers by virtue of outstanding performance or conspicuous gallantry. They were not accompanied by an increase in salary or a permanent promotion to the higher level. Dragoons were relatively heavily armed cavalry who generally fought dismounted. By 1863 it was recognized that a lightly armed and highly mobile force had a marked advantage over the

dragoon in conducting reconnaissance and raids behind enemy lines.

7. Lewis F. Roe, "Recitals and Reminiscences: With Canby at Valverde," *National Tribune* (Washington, D.C.), November 3, 1910 (courtesy Jerry Thompson).

8. In his testimony to Congress in July 1863, Colonel Benjamin Roberts noted that the reason there were so many disloyal officers in New Mexico was that all of the loyal officers had been withdrawn for service elsewhere. The loss of officers was also apparent in the ranks ("Report of the Joint Committee on the Conduct of the War," Senate Document 108, 37th Cong., 3d sess., vol. 3 (1863), pp. 364–72). Lewis Roe (Company F, Seventh U.S. Infantry) reported that "we were being deserted by our officers...we were practically an army without officers." Roe, "Recitals and Reminiscences."

9. Although no firsthand accounts of the Sibley–Davis meeting have survived, the rationale for Sibley's New Mexico campaign is discussed in several sources: Charles Walker, "Causes of the Confederate Invasion of New Mexico," *New Mexico Historical Review* 8 (1967), pp. 171–72; Latham Anderson's article "Canby's Services in the New Mexico Campaign," in Johnson and Buel, *Battles and Leaders*; Trevanion Teel's article "Sibley's New Mexico Campaign" in *Battles and Leaders*; and Robert Twitchell's *Leading Facts of New Mexico History*, vol. 2 (Cedar Rapids: Torch Press, 1912). Anderson notes that the gold supply of the "Pacific Coast [was] a source of strength considered by Mr. Lincoln to be essential to the successful prosecution of the war." E. B. Long provides an additional summary of the Civil War politics in the West. E. B. Long, "War Beyond the River." Zamonski describes other attempts to capture Colorado gold for the South. Stanley Zamonski, "Colorado Gold and the Confederacy," in Numa L. James, ed., *The 1956 Brand Book of the Denver Posse of the Westerners* (Boulder: Johnson Publishing, 1957), pp. 87–117.

10. Raymond McCoy debunks the frequently recounted story of the Federals filling their canteens with contraband whiskey and brandy in "Victory at Fort Fillmore" *New Mexico Magazine* (August 1961), p. 20. He notes that the story apparently was originated some twenty-three years after the fact by an unnamed bugler from Company B of the Fifth New Mexico Volunteers, a company not even reported to be present at Fort Fillmore. He further notes that there are no Confederate reports of drunken Federal soldiers.

11. Union and Confederate armies were modeled after the pre-Victorian, Napoleonic armies of Europe. J. B. Lippincott, *U.S. Infantry Tactics for the Instruction, Exercise, and Maneuvers of the United States Infantry* (Philadelphia: J. B. Lippincott and Co., 1861). The basic military formation was the *company*.

Companies were commanded by captains and consisted of two *platoons*, each led by a junior officer or subaltern who was usually a first or second lieutenant. Platoons consisted of two *sections* of about ten to twenty men each (this number varied greatly among regiments, typically with more men in a company at the beginning of the war). At the base of this pyramid-like structure were *comrades-in-battle*, something like the contemporary buddy system, consisting of groups of four men. An infantry company had a fully authorized strength of ninety-seven men. More typically, companies had forty to eighty men.

Companies composed *regiments*, commanded by colonels. Per Arthur L. Wagner, *Organization and Tactics* (New York: Westerman and Co., 1895), the "tactical unit" in the Civil War was the regiment:

> The 'tactical unit' is the largest body of troops that can be directly commanded by a single leader, and, at the same time, be able to appear in close order on the battlefield without risk of quickly incurring ruinous losses from enemy fire.

Although "the book" called for ten companies per regiment, regiments were usually "fleshed out" with eight companies. At the beginning of the war, regiments typically had upwards of eight hundred men. However, as the war progressed and death and desertion took their toll, regimental rolls fell precipitously. By the spring of 1863, the average Union regiment mustered 425 effectives.

The primary military maneuver element was the *brigade*, commanded by a brigadier general. The number of regiments in a brigade varied from two to six, with an average of four. Until early 1863, between two and six brigades were combined into a *division*, commanded by a major general. As many as four divisions (but typically three) composed an army *corps*, commanded by a lieutenant general. Corps were grouped into *armies* (for example, the Army of the Potomac, the Army of Northern Virginia, and so forth) commanded by generals. (In 1863 General Joseph Hooker changed the structure to eliminate one level of command structure.)

On the Confederate side, the number of men composing the ranks of regiments, brigades, and so forth varied, but typically held more than their Union counterparts.

12. The life of Edward Canby is detailed in Max Heyman's book, *The Prudent Soldier* (Glendale: Arthur H. Clark Publishers, 1959).

13. There was a widespread belief among the Union enlisted men that Canby and Sibley were brothers-in-law. This belief may have strengthened resentment of Canby's cautious behavior during the New Mexico campaign. Although not much is known about Canby's wife, both men's biographers dismiss as groundless the rumor of a relationship by marriage, although an allegation that Canby was the best man at Sibley's wedding persists. It is clear, however, that the two men were well acquainted and probably considered themselves to be friends before Fort Sumter.

14. James L. Collins, letter sent Feb. 11, 1862, to Wm. Dole, U.S. Commissioner of Indian Affairs. Letters Received by the Office of Indian Affairs, RG 75, NA.

15. *The War of the Rebellion: A Compilation of the Official Records of the Union and Confederate Armies* 128 vol. (Washington, D.C., 1880–1901), series I, vol. 9, pp. 643–44.

16. Roe, "Recitals and Reminiscences."

17. Fort Craig was named for Louis S. Craig, a captain in the Third U.S. Infantry who had been killed by deserters in 1852. Marion C. Grinstead, *Life and Death of a Frontier Fort: Fort Craig, New Mexico, 1854–1885* (Socorro: Socorro County Historical Society, 1973).

18. The last of these "scouts" down the Pecos before the Battle of Valverde was conducted by Captain Julius C. Shaw and ten men of the Fourth New Mexico Volunteers between January 1 and January 17, 1862.

19. The Confederates who had controlled southern New Mexico since the summer of 1861 also had their share of Indian problems. Colonel Baylor was bothered by Apaches in 1861 and 1862. A. W. Evans, "Canby at Valverde," in Johnson and Buel, *Battles and Leaders*, p. 699.

20. OR, I: 4, p. 89.

21. Jerry D. Thompson, *Westward the Texans: The Civil War Journal of Private William Randolph Howell* (El Paso: Texas Western Press, 1990), p. 85. Most regimental structures show Teel's company as the artillery arm of Baylor's Command (the Second Regiment of Texas Mounted Rifles). However, Teel essentially operated independently as Sibley's artillery commander throughout the New Mexico campaign. Although his official report of the Battle of Valverde is not explicit (OR, I: 9, pp. 523–25), it strongly implies that he commanded a two-section battery of six-pounder guns. One two-gun section was commanded by Lieutenant James Bradford and the other two-gun section by Lieutenants Jordan Bennett and Joseph McGuiness.

22. Nolie Mumey, *Bloody Trails along the Rio Grande—A Day-by-Day Diary of Alonzo Ferdinand Ickis* (Denver: Old West Publishing Company, 1958), p. 72.

Chapter 3

1. Smith says that the camp was fifteen miles south of Fort Craig, but this is apparently a misassessment, since he notes that the corps traveled some twenty-seven miles on the thirteenth, fifteenth, and seventeenth before getting within sight of the fort. W. A. Faulkner "With Sibley in New Mexico—The Journal of William Henry Smith," *West Texas Historical Association Yearbook 27* (October 1951), p. 133. The life of Tom Green has been documented by Odie Faulk in *General Tom Green—Fightin' Texan* (Waco: Texian Press, 1963).

2. *San Antonio Herald* (May 6, 1856), quoting the *New Orleans Bee* (courtesy Jerry Thompson).

3. Thompson, *Westward the Texans*, p. 86; Baylor's command was a battalion of the Second Regiment of Texas Mounted Rifles.

4. Faulkner, "With Sibley in New Mexico," p. 134.

5. Ezra J. Warner, *Generals in Grey* (Baton Rouge: Louisiana State University Press, 1959), pp. 270–71.

6. Theophilius Noel, *A Campaign from Santa Fe to the Mississippi—Being a History of the Old Sibley Brigade* (1865; repr., Raleigh: Whittet and Shepperson Press, 1961), p. 15. February 12 was also memorable for Theophilius Noel as the day when he first noticed the symptoms of small-pox, a disease that would keep him from accompanying the Sibley Brigade on its ill-fated invasion.

7. Jacqueline D. Meketa, ed., *Legacy of Honor—The Life of Rafael Chacón* (Albuquerque: University of New Mexico Press, 1986), pp. 144–45.

8. Ickis says "1,000 whites and 2,000 Greasers," which would leave at most a few hundred men manning the fort (Mumey, *Bloody Trails*, p. 73).

9. OR, I: 9, p. 632.

10. Letters from H. J. Hunter to Jettie Word (courtesy Jerry Thompson).

11. The Fifth Regiment's companies were D, E, F, H, I, and K. Teel remained behind with companies A, B, C, and G (Thompson, *Westward the Texans*, p. 86).

12. Thompson, *Westward the Texans*, p. 86; OR, I: 9, p. 632; OR, I: 9, pp. 630–31. Based on a service record entry for Anastacia Gonzales of Company A of the Third New Mexico Volunteers, that unit may have been the one "captured" by the Confederates on Thursday (Compiled Service Records of the Third New Mexico Volunteers, RG 94, M427, Rolls 38–39, NA).

13. Ebenezer Hanna, *Journal of Ebenezer Hanna* (Texas State Archives), p. 1.

14. Faulkner, "With Sibley in New Mexico," p. 134.

15. Hanna, *Journal*, p. 1.

16. Stephen B. Oates, *Confederate Cavalry West of the River* (Austin: University of Texas Press, 1961), pp. 60–61.

17. Faulkner, "With Sibley in New Mexico," p. 134; Dee Brecheisen of Peralta, New Mexico has located some of the Texan campsites in Simons Canyon.

18. Mumey, *Bloody Trails*, p. 74. It has been suggested by some that Sibley should have attempted to block this important supply train and that his mobile force was ideally suited to do so. This would have gained supplies for the Texans and denied those same supplies to the Union troops at Fort Craig. This may reflect inadequate reconnaissance on Sibley's part (that is, he did not find out about the train soon enough) or poor strategy. In either case, there is no Confederate mention of the Fort Craig wagon train in the official reports on the engagement.

19. Darlis Miller, "Hispanos and the Civil War in New Mexico," *New Mexico Historical Review 54* (1979), p. 108.

20. Faulkner, "With Sibley in New Mexico," p. 134.

21. Immediately prior to the Battle of Valverde, Colonel Canby organized his forces into five columns (OR, I: 9, pp. 630-31). However, he did not follow this order of battle rigorously on February 20–21, 1862. Therefore, I have chosen to show the Union order of battle by type rather than in the column alignment throughout.

22. Jerry Thompson has detailed Graydon's colorful life in *Desert Tiger: Captain Paddy Graydon and the Civil War in the Far Southwest* (El Paso: Texas Western Press, 1992). The apple-peddler incident is described on p. 32.

23. Standard infantry tactics of the time called for skirmishers to be deployed up to a few hundred yards forward of the main line of battle in groups of four (so-called comrades-in-battle), with each man five paces apart and the groups of four no more than forty paces from their neighbors. Typically, skirmishers, were controlled by bugle calls (Lippincott, *U.S. Infantry Tactics*, pp. 155–89). Skirmish lines were common in the nineteenth century, having been used to screen the main body of troops under both Napoleonic and Mexican War battle schemes. McWhiney and Jamieson, *Attack and Die* (Tuscaloosa: University of Alabama Press, 1982), pp. 32–33. However, according to Stewart, in *Picket's Charge—A Microhistory of the Final Charge at Gettysburg* (Boston: Houghton Mifflin, 1959, 1987), p. 65:

In the history of tactics, the skirmish line must be considered a temporary expedient, reaching its height of usefulness under the particular conditions of this war [the Civil War]. Its importance sprang from the increased range of in-fantry small arms. In an attack, the traditional battle line—men advancing in two ranks, elbow-to-elbow—had become almost an anachronism, and in a sense had to be protected by skirmishers. In a static situation, unless you had a skirmish line, the enemy's sharpshooters would work up close. The only solution was to send out skirmishers of your own to keep the enemy at a distance and also to protect against surprise attack.

Griffith also discusses the use of skirmishers in Civil War battle tactics, in *Battle Tactics of the Civil War* (New Haven: Yale University Press, 1987).

24. Thompson, *Desert Tiger*, p. 34.

25. Mumey, *Bloody Trails*, p. 74.

26. Ovando Hollister, *Boldly They Rode* (Lakewood: Golden Press, 1949), p. 101.

27. In his letter to Wm. Dole of March 1, 1862, James L. Collins details the engagement on February sixteenth.

Chapter 4

1. Faulkner, *With Sibley in New Mexico*, p. 134.

2. According to Marshall and Walt (*Rio Abajo*, pp. 240–41, 279), Paraje was located at or near the site of the pre-Revolt village of Fra Cristobal and the two names were apparently used interchangeably in the 1860s.

3. Mumey, *Bloody Trails*, p. 71.

4. Ibid., p. 74.

5. Collins, letter of March 1, 1862; Maximiano Madril's recollections are described in a 1956 *Albuquerque Tribune* article by Howard Bryan ("Off the Beaten Path," August 30, 1956, p. 33). A detailed analysis of Paraje de Fra Cristobal is given by Douglas Boyd in *Paraje*

de Fra Cristobal: Investigation of a Territorial Period Hispanic Village Site in Southern New Mexico (Amarillo: U.S. Department of the Interior, Bureau of Reclamation, 1986).

6. Collins describes the movement on February 19 to the eastern highlands; Wesche details the arrival of the Second New Mexico Militia on February 19 and 20. Jerry Thompson, "The Civil War Diary of Major Charles Emil Wesche," *Password* 39 (Spring 1994) pp. 37–47. See also Mumey, *Bloody Trails*, p. 75.

7. It seems likely that Chacón and his men had located the graves of Private Kemp and perhaps other non-combat casualties rather than any battle casualties. Confederate reports and diaries specifically note that there were no Confederate casualties on the sixteenth.

8. Noel, *Campaign*, p. 18.

9. Hall, *Sibley's New Mexico Campaign*, p. 80, and Collins (March 1, 1862) say that some of the wagons were abandoned along the route and burned during the night of February 20 by Federal "spies." Noel (*Campaign*, p. 18) suggests that at least part of the Confederate train may have continued northward, toward Valverde, throughout the night. This is not mentioned in other reports; however, since all of Noel's reports are at best second-hand, it may be a confusion with the stragglers from Paraje mentioned by Hall and Collins.

10. Canby's command included four different categories of soldiers: regular army (infantry, cavalry, and artillery), New Mexico Volunteers (infantry and cavalry), New Mexico Militia (infantry), and Colorado Volunteers (infantry). The volunteers had enlisted in the Federal service for periods of up to three years and had received some basic training. The militia were hastily recruited, unorganized, and virtually untrained soldiers in service to the territorial government, not the federal government. (Although, as noted by Wesche, the militamen were "mustered into the service of the United States" by a commissioned officer when they arrived at Fort Craig—see Thompson, "Civil War Diary," p. 43.)

11. The topography shown in Canby's map south of the mesa is incorrect. The arroyos south of Mesa del Contadero actually run almost east–west rather than northeast–southwest as depicted.

12. Collins, letter dated March 1, 1862.

13. David B. Gracy, ed., "New Mexico Campaign Letters of Frank Starr: 1861–1862," *Texas Military History 4* (Fall 1964), p. 172.

Civil War artillery consisted of two sets of vehicles. The first set of vehicles included the gun on its carriage attached to a hitch on a two-wheeled vehicle called a limber, which also carried an ammunition chest. The second set of vehicles consisted of a limber with a single ammunition chest and a caisson, another two-wheeled vehicle that carried two ammunition chests, assorted tools, and a spare wheel. Each of the two-vehicle combinations was drawn by a four or six-horse team and had a nine-man gun crew. Dean S. Thomas, *Cannons—An Introduction to Civil War Artillery* (Gettysburg: Thomas Publishing, 1985), pp. 11–12.

The Confederates had two types of artillery at the Battle of Valverde: six-pounder field guns with a range of about fifteen hundred yards and twelve-pounder "light" howitzers. I have assumed that these "light" howitzers were actually mountain howitzers, much lighter cannons with a range of only nine hundred yards, which may have been captured by Baylor from the Federal forces at San Augustin Springs and Cooks Canyon. This would be consistent with a brigade designed to move quickly over potentially rough terrain. Mountain howitzers were designed to be pulled directly by a single horse or a mule without limbers. These cannons could also be disassembled and packed directly onto three pack animals to cover ground that might be inaccessible to wheeled vehicles.

The process of attaching cannons and

caissons to limber carts was known as "limber-ing" or "limbering up" (Thomas, *Cannons*, pp. 27, 32).

The limbers, caissons, and so forth associ-ated with each gun constituted an artillery platoon, normally commanded by a sergeant. Two guns constituted a section, normally commanded by a lieutenant. Four to six guns comprised a battery, normally commanded by a captain.

14. Meketa, *Legacy of Honor*, pp. 148, 166.

15. Sibley estimated that the Federal forces opposing him on the twentieth exceeded twenty-five hundred. This is, in all likelihood, too high (OR, I: 9, p. 507).

16. OR, I: 9, p. 489.

17. OR, I: 9, p. 637; Meketa, *Legacy of Honor*, p. 166, Gracy; "New Mexico Campaign Letters, p. 172.

18. Mumey, *Bloody Trails*, p. 75. The Colo-rado Volunteers had been mustered into Federal service at Canon City, Colorado on October 27, 1861, and had been detailed to support Canby's forces in New Mexico. They left Canon City on December 5, 1861 and arrived at Fort Craig on February 3, 1862 (Mumey, *Bloody Trails*, p. 30). The company that fought at Valverde is vari-ously reported as "Captain Dodd's Independent Company," "Company A of the Second Colo-rado Infantry," and "Company A of the Colo-rado Volunteers." There may also have been some men from Company B of the same regiment.

19. Ezra Warner, *Generals in Blue* (Baton Rouge: Louisiana State University Press, 1964, 1992), pp. 405–6; *Dictionary of American Biography, vol. 16* (New York: Charles Scribner's Sons, 1990), p. 2; and *The National Cyclopedia of American Biography, vol. 5* (New York: James T. White and Co., 1907), pp. 55–56.

20. Dee Brechiesen of Peralta, New Mexico, has located the remains of these entrenchments on the east bank of the river across from Fort Craig. He has also located the site of the Confederate camp on the bluff above the river.

21. Wesche reported that his infantrymen camped in the post corral just southwest of the fort while his cavalry camped in the bottomland below the fort (Thompson, "Civil War Diary," p. 42).

22. *U.S. Army Regulations*, 1861; *Field Manual*, pp. 74–80; The fact that, on the morning of February 21, Lieutenant Colonel Scurry of the Fourth Regiment was unaware that Sibley had dispatched Pyron of Baylor's command to the ford is perhaps suggestive of a large camp with a west–east layout (for ex-ample, Fourth, Fifth, Seventh, Baylor). In addition, since the mules of the Fourth Regi-ment stampeded, it is plausible to assume that they were picketed closest to the river.

23. Confederate camp food is discussed in Oates (*Confederate Cavalry*, pp. 53–54). Hanna notes that the camp on February 20 was dry and wood-poor (Hanna, *Journal*, p. 3).

24. Letter from Robert Scott to C. A. Dupree, dated April 10, 1925 (courtesy Steven Dupree); this is also noted by Mamie Yeary in *Reminis-cences of the Boys in Grey* (1912; repr., Dayton: Morningside Press, 1986), p. 667. The Yeary treatise is a collection of interviews with Confederate veterans in various retirement and nursing homes conducted in the early twentieth century. Included were interviews with more than forty of Sibley's men.

25. The story of Graydon's midnight raid, felt by many to be one of the myths of Valverde, is told in several references, although there is no mention of it in any of the official reports of the battle. The multiple references all seem to stem from a single report (George Pettis, "The Confederate Invasion of New Mexico and Arizona," in Johnson and Buel, *Battles and Leaders*, vol. 2, p. 105n), and it is conceivable that neither Sibley nor Canby would have been particularly proud of this escapade and so would have omitted it from their official reports. In his account of the incident, Bell

suggests that Graydon, whom he calls "Pat Gorman," failed because of his limited knowledge of pyrotechnics, and the system went off prematurely before the poor mules could reach the camp. Joseph M. Bell, "The Campaign of New Mexico, 1862," in *War Papers Read before the Commandery of the State of Wisconsin, Military Order of the Loyal Legion of the United States,* vol. 1 (Milwaukee: Burdick, Armitage and Allen, 1891), pp. 57–58. Thompson notes that "regardless of the facts," such a raid would have been consistent with "Graydon's widely acknowledged reputation for the spectacular" (Thompson, *Desert Tiger*, pp. 35–36).

26. Whatever the initiating event, the stampede of the Confederate mules and their subsequent roundup by Union troopers is well documented and combined with the losses on February 21, led to Sibley's order to destroy a significant portion of his supply train at the dry camp. C.S.A. estimates of the loss of animals were 150 (Gracy, "New Mexico Campaign Letters," p. 172), Federal counts were two hundred to three hundred (OR, I: 9, p. 489). Ickis gives a precise number of 164 (Mumey, *Bloody Trails*, p. 75).

The half moon rose at 1:00 A.M. and was high in the southern sky at 5:54 A.M., about one hour before sunrise on February 21, 1862. (This and other astronomical information courtesy of Dr. Bob Victor of Michigan State University's Abrams Planetarium.)

Chapter 5

1. The Baylor–Sibley feud is well documented in Thompson's biography (Thompson, *Henry Hopkins Sibley*, pp. 315–19) and Hall's article, "Planter vs. Frontiersman: Conflict in Confederate Indian Policy," in Frank E. Vandiver's *Essays on the American Civil War* (Austin: University of Texas Press, 1968), pp. 45–72.

Some reports state that Pyron took 250 men to the ford. However, his own report says that he left with 180 (OR, I: 9, p. 512).

2. Mars rose at 3:18 A.M. and was about twenty-one degrees above the southeastern horizon at 5:45 A.M. on February 21. Chacón reports seeing the sunrise (Meketa, *Legacy of Honor*, p. 167) and Hanna notes that the morning of the twenty-first was cold and cloudy (Faulkner, "With Sibley in New Mexico," p. 135).

3. There were three fordable areas immediately north of Mesa del Contadero. I refer to these as the lower ford, the middle ford, and the upper ford. The first of these was immediately above the right-angle bend in the river just north of the mesa. This is also referred to by some as the San Marcial ford. The middle ford is a broader area stretching about three hundred yards and lying about eight hundred yards north of the lower ford at the gentle bend to the east. The upper ford lies another few hundred yards further upriver.

4. This gentleman, who is not identified by name, was captured by Union forces during his quest and exchanged after the battle. Don Alberts, *Rebels on the Rio Grande: The Civil War Journal of A. B. Peticolas* (Albuquerque: University of New Mexico Press, 1984), p. 49.

5. Alberts, *Rebels*, p. 41; F. Stanley, *The Civil War in New Mexico* (Denver: The World Press, 1960), p. 248; F. Stanley, *Fort Craig* (Pampa: Pampa Print Shop, 1963), p. 61.

6. OR, I: 9, p. 489.

7. Companies C, D, G, and K of the Third U.S. Cavalry and Company G of the First U.S. Cavalry.

8. Companies assigned to Captains Pedro Sanchez, Juan Sarracino, Ricardo Branch, and Rafael Chacón.

9. The number and type of guns in McRae's battery are variously reported. In "The Guns of Valverde," *Password 5* (1960), pp. 21–34, McMaster and Ruhlen conclude, based on post

returns and various correspondence, that there were four twelve-pounder light howitzers and two six-pounder guns. However, an article in the San Antonio *Herald* noted by Martin H. Hall, in *The Confederate Army of New Mexico* (Austin: The Presidial Press, 1978), p. 289, says that there were "two twelve-pounder field pieces, three six-pounder guns and one twelve-pounder howitzer." The post-battle post return from Fort Craig states that the battery was comprised of three 6-pounder guns, two 12-pounder field howitzers, and one 12-pounder mountain howitzer. I have chosen to use these numbers even though the McMaster and Ruhlen evaluation suggests that the mountain howitzer had been removed in January.

Canby describes the movement of McRae's cannons to the ford—two sections with Roberts in the morning and one section in the afternoon (OR, I: 9, pp. 487–93). In *Destiny at Valverde: The Life and Death of Alexander McRae* (Socorro: Socorro Historical Society, 1992), p. 35, Grinstead suggests that McRae himself went to the ford with Roberts.

10. Company K of the Fifth U.S. Infantry (Brotherton), Company H of the Seventh U.S. Infantry (Ingraham), Company A of the Third New Mexico Volunteers (Captain William Mortimore), and Company B of the Fifth New Mexico Volunteers (Captain Santiago Hubbell).

11. Probably Company G under Captain Robert Morris.

12. OR, I: 9, p. 497.

13. Meketa, *Legacy of Honor*, p. 167. Duncan states that he left Fort Craig at 8:00 A.M. (OR, I: 9, p. 497), but this report is inconsistent with Roberts, Scurry, Pyron, and Chacón, so I have assumed that Duncan was in error. Sunrise at the Valverde ford would have been between 6:45 and 6:55 (sunrise on the horizon was at 6:43, so it would have been a few minutes later for an observer in the river bottom with the mesa lying to the east–southeast). The two companies that Duncan found at the ford are assumed to

have been Chacón's and Graydon's.

14. Thompson, *Henry Hopkins Sibley*, p. 271.

15. The Brigands, also called the "Santa Fe Gamblers," are described by Josephy as "an unseemly pack of frontier gunmen, thieves, and unattached ne'er-do-wells who had been collected in the Mesilla Valley" (Josephy, *Civil War in the American West*, p. 59). Stanley (*Fort Craig*, p. 62) says that Phillips was dispatched to Scurry at "8 minutes to 9 am." However, this seems about one hour too late.

16. Meketa, *Legacy of Honor*, p. 167.

17. Companies B, E, G, and H of the Fourth Regiment. Note that in the Official Reports, Raguet's name is consistently misspelled "Ragnet."

18. Unpublished Raguet genealogy ("The Raguet Family") (courtesy Jerry Thompson).

19. OR, I: 9, p. 524.

20. Chacón says that Morris didn't cross the river until about 9:00 A.M. with Valdez following at about 9:30, and that Roberts arrived first with his artillery. This is inconsistent with the reports of both Roberts and Duncan. Because their reports were written immediately after the battle, I have chosen them as a more credible sources at this level of detail than Chacón, who penned his account several years later.

21. According to Ickis (Mumey, *Bloody Trails*, pp. 85–86), who toured the top of the mesa and the battlefield a few days after the fight, there were seven parallel sand embankments or ridges between fifty and one hundred yards apart.

22. The term "minié ball" does not refer to the size of the round, but to a French officer, Claude Étienne Minié of the Chasseurs d'Orleans, who invented the hollow-base, conical projectile. When fired, gases expanded into the hollow base, forcing the bullet into the lands or rifling in the barrel of the gun. The resulting spin stabilized the bullet in flight, permitting significantly longer ranges and increased accuracy.

23. The Model 1841 .54 caliber "Mississippi"

rifle was so-named because Jefferson Davis's Mississippi Volunteers used it in the Mexican War. It used a round ball.

The percussion system of ignition came into use in the U.S. in 1841, with the U.S. Percussion Musket, Model 1841. Many of these .69 caliber smoothbores were rifled early in the 1850s and became the U.S. Minié rifle, .69 caliber. Information courtesy of Charles Meketa, who has made a detailed evaluation of Civil War–vintage Union military hardware in New Mexico. He and Jacqueline Meketa documented the smoothbore modification process in *One Blanket and Ten Days Rations* (Globe: Southwest Parks and Monument Association, 1980), pp. 14–15. These armament details are also supported by Wallen's report and by a letter from Francisco Abreu (First New Mexico Volunteers) to Major B. C. Cutler, dated June 27, 1865 (Wallen and Abreu correspondence courtesy Charles Meketa).

24. Oates, *Confederate Cavalry*, pp. 62–63.

25. Yeary, *Reminiscences*, pp. 760–61.

26. Both Oates (*Confederate Cavalry*, p. 86) and McWhiney (*Attack and Die*, p. 136) suggests that the Confederates followed standard cavalry tactics, which had one man in four designated to hold the horses. Later in the battle, however, the Texans simply tied their horses, probably because they felt that they were outnumbered.

27. Duncan describes one six-pounder and one piece of artillery, but Teel and the six-pounders did not arrive until about 11:00 A.M., so the other cannon noted by Duncan may have been the second of Reily's guns.

28. Roberts commended Meinhold in his report on the battle (OR, I: 9, p. 496). Meinhold's anti-secessionist adventures were described by Roberts in his testimony before Congress in July 1862.

29. George Cook, "Letter from the Front," *New Mexico Magazine* (September 1965) pp. 2–3.

30. The 440 does not include the 150 men assigned to hold the horses near the river.

31. Alexander McRae's colorful life and untimely death have been chronicled by Grinstead in *Destiny at Valverde*.

32. Gracy, "New Mexico Campaign Letters," p. 173.

33. OR, I: 9, p. 494.

34. In a series of very pointed letters, Roberts all but accused Duncan of dereliction of duty because of his failure to take the bosque. Although Duncan maintained that he had asked permission to do so "several times," but had not been so ordered, Roberts noted that he had ordered Duncan to go where he now said that he was requesting to go at least three times. He further asked the names of Duncan's alleged messengers so he could "arrest and punish them for not conveying the orders" (OR, I: 9, pp. 499–502). In retrospect, it is by no means clear that Duncan's slight numerical advantage would have been sufficient to compensate for the natural defensive position occupied by the Texans, even with the help of McRae's and Hall's artillery, and he may have worried about being flanked if he acted too rashly. However, Roberts's righteous indignation is a bit surprising considering that he did not enforce his orders more forcefully. The ignoring of a critical command by a subordinate simply cannot go unnoticed. The Roberts–Duncan affair may never be completely resolved.

35. W. W. Mills's article, in *Galveston Weekly News*, dated November 29, 1883 (courtesy Jerry Thompson).

36. OR, I: 9, p. 524.

37. There are several discrepancies concerning the number of C.S.A. artillery pieces and their initial arrival and disposition at Valverde. Although Starr (Gracy, "New Mexico Campaign Letters," p. 172) refers to "15 pieces of artillery" (four six-pounder guns under Teel and, by implication, eleven twelve-pounder mountain howitzers), only twelve seem to have been involved at Valverde. Four of these were Teel's

six-pounders and the others seem to have been four twelve-pounders under Lieutenant John Reily of the Fourth Regiment and four twelve-pounders under Lieutenant William Wood of the Fifth Regiment. Hall (*Confederate Army*, pp. 128, 211) suggests that only one section (two guns) from each of these regimental artillery batteries actually may have been moved to the ford. This is consistent with Teel's report (OR, I: 9, pp. 523–25) and Canby's report (OR, I: 9, pp. 487–93). None of Canby's battle maps show more than six C.S.A. cannons and neither of Chacón's maps shows more than five. Therefore, I assume that eight guns were brought to the ford and that the other four were left with the train.

Peticolas (Alberts, *Rebels*, p. 42) states that Teel, with five pieces, arrived at Pyron's location about ten minutes after the cavalrymen of the Fourth Texas had taken up their positions. Teel himself says that he arrived with two pieces under Lieutenant James Bradford at that time and was reinforced by four more pieces under Bennett and McGuinness "some time later" (OR, I: 9, pp. 523–25). The account of Frank Starr, an artilleryman with Reily's battery, generally confirms the Teel/Peticolas account (Gracy, "New Mexico Campaign Letters," pp. 172–73). Scurry says that Teel arrived at 1:00 P.M. and Raguet says 12:00 noon, but both agree that Teel arrived after Scurry had reached the field. Pyron says he fought for about three hours before Teel's arrival. This places Teel's artillery at the field between 10:30 and 11:00. This estimate is not inconsistent with Alberts's estimate of 11:00 P.M. (Alberts, *Rebels*, p. 42n4).

Raguet and Starr both state that Reily's artillery was ordered to proceed with Raguet to reinforce Pyron (OR, I: 9, pp. 516–18; Gracy, "New Mexico Campaign Letters," p. 173). However, it is clear from both reports that they lagged behind, especially Starr's gun that had a "broken-down" team.

The guns of the Fifth Regiment, under Lieutenant Wood, left camp with Green at about noon (OR, I: 9, pp. 518–22) and probably arrived at the ford between 1:30 and 1:45.

38. Although the top of Mesa del Contadero commands the entire battlefield as well as the route of the Confederate train, it would not have been usable by artillery or large bodies of troops. Therefore, it is reasonable to assume that no fighting would have occurred here, but that scouts and signalmen would have used the elevation to their advantage. In fact, Ickis (Mumey, *Bloody Trails*, p. 85) specifically states that some of Graydon's men operated atop the mesa on the twenty-first.

While there is no direct evidence of the Union communication system at Valverde, it is plausible to assume that Canby had a semaphore signal station on the southwest edge of the mesa, with a clear line-of-sight to the fort, from which he could receive near-real-time information about activities east and north of the mesa. (Note that heliographs, which frequently have been associated with military communications on the frontier, were not introduced until the late 1870s.) Using a semaphore system, Canby almost certainly would have been aware of Raguet's reinforcement of Pyron no more than fifteen minutes after Raguet's arrival at the sand embankment. (See Alberts, *Rebels*, p. 41, and Wesche's report in OR, I: 53, p. 452, for hints of the communication system used at Valverde.)

39. Green says that during the morning his forces were deployed in a position to "threaten the fort from the south side of the Mesa" (OR, I: 9, p. 519). However, neither Canby nor Plympton (who was with Selden south of the mesa until the late morning) make any mention of an engagement south of the mesa in the morning. In fact, the only documented engagement south of the mesa during the entire day was Wesche and Pino's uneventful "encounter" with two companies of Texans in the early afternoon (Thompson, "Civil War Diary," p.

43). Therefore, I conclude that Green and the Fifth and Seventh regiments probably remained high on the bluffs near the Confederate camp until ordered to the ford by Sibley.

40. Wingate's battalion of the Fifth Infantry (Companies B, D, F, and I) and Plympton's battalion (Companies C and F of the Seventh Infantry and A and H of the Tenth Infantry).

41. Recall that the eighth company, Company K under Rafael Chacón, was already at the ford operating with Duncan.

42. Alberts, *Rebels*, p. 42.

43. OR, I: 9, p. 514.

44. OR, I: 9, p. 514; Alberts, *Rebels*, p. 43; Gracy, "New Mexico Campaign Letters," p. 173.

Chapter 6

1. Companies C, D, G, and K of the Third Cavalry; Company G of the First Cavalry; five companies of New Mexico Volunteers (Sanchez, Sarracino, Branch, Chacón, and Barrientos); and Company K of the Fifth Infantry (David Brotherton).

2. Pyron's total losses, excluding Teel's battery but including those suffered in the final charge, were only three killed and seven wounded. Raguet's total for the day were eleven killed or mortally wounded and twenty-three wounded (see Appendix), but most of these were probably suffered in his abortive afternoon charge. Collins's report of twenty Union casualties prior to 1:00 P.M. may be in reference to Duncan's losses on the right (Collins, March 1, 1862).

3. Chacón says this occurred at 10:00 A.M. but I am inclined to go with Roberts and Duncan's estimates. (See also n. 5 below.)

4. OR, I: 9, p. 495.

5. Carson states that he arrived at the ford at about 9:00 A.M. and gradually advanced up the west bank as the Texans expanded their line to the north, until ordered by Canby to cross the river at about 1:00 P.M. (OR, I: 9, p. 502). However, Canby did not even arrive at the ford until about 2:45, and Canby himself states that he ordered Carson to move to the ford (1) after Selden had been so ordered and (2) after he was convinced that Sibley was committed to the ford. Similarly, Roberts notes that Selden and Carson did not arrive at the ford until after McRae's battery had opened fire, which he places at 10:00 A.M. For these reasons, I conclude that Carson and Selden both reported to Roberts at the ford at about noon.

6. OR, I: 9, p. 519.

7. OR, I: 9, p. 523.

8. OR, I: 9, p. 519.

9. I have deduced the following noontime Confederate company locations from the official records:

Fourth Regiment

A (Hardeman)	Right with Scurry
B (Scarborough)	Left with Raguet
C (Hampton)	Right with Scurry
D (Leseur)	Right with Scurry
E (Buckholts)	Left with Raguet
F (Crosson)	Right with Scurry
G (van den Heuvel)	Left with Raguet
H (Alexander)	Left with Raguet
I (Nunn)	Right with Scurry
K (Foard)	Right with Scurry
Artillery (Reily)	Left-center with Green

Fifth Regiment

A (Shropshire)	Center/left with Lockridge
B (Lang)	Center/right with Lockridge
C (Shannon)	With train
D (Ragsdale)	Center/left with Lockridge
E (McPhaill)	Far left with McNeill
F (Campbell)	Center/left with Lockridge
G (McCown)	Center/right with Lockridge

H (Pridgen)	With train
I (Killough)	Far left with McNeill
K (Jordan)	Far left with McNeill
Artillery (Wood)	Right with Scurry

Seventh Regiment

A (Jordan)	With Train
B (Hoffmann)	With Train
F (Wiggins)	With Train
H (Adair)	With Train
I (Gardner)	With Train

Baylor's Command (Pyron)

B (Jett)	Left Center
D (Walker)	Left Center
E (Stafford)	Left Center
San Elizaro (Nicholson)	Left Center
Arizona Rangers (Frazier)	Left Center
Brigands (Phillips)	Left Center
Artillery (Teel)	Various

10. OR, I: 9, p. 517.

11. Chacón implies that the Texans fled under his attack, abandoning the piece (Meketa, *Legacy of Honor*, p. 168).

12. See Chapter 5, n. 37.

13. OR, I: 9, p. 523.

14. OR, I: 53, p. 452. This action probably preceded the movement of Sutton to the ford since he left only three companies with the train.

15. Canby says that the company that accompanied him to the ford was G of the First U.S. Cavalry; but unless the First Cavalry was operating in independent squadrons, this is at odds with both Roberts and Duncan, who reported that Claflin (in command of G of the First) went to the ford during Roberts's early morning deployment.

16. Biographical information on Paul is taken from *The National Cyclopedia of American Biography*, vol. 12, pp. 242–43 and Warner, *Generals in Blue*, pp. 363–64.

17. The detachment left at Fort Craig was probably comprised of Company A of the Fourth New Mexico Volunteers under Colonel Paul and Captain Julius Shaw and one or two companies of the Third New Mexico Volunteers, probably H under Captain Pablo Martínez and K under Tomás Valencia. This assessment is based on a process of elimination using the Official Reports and eliminating groups known to be in action at Valverde or south of the mesa. In addition, about seven hundred militia and "some regulars" remained.

18. Chacón says that this occurred at 10:00 A.M. rather than at 12:30 P.M.; Roberts suggests that Selden didn't arrive at the lower ford until 12:00 noon.

19. Alberts, *Rebels*, p. 43. Peticolas also noted the intermittent snow showers (p. 51). Although he says that they occurred in the morning, he associated them with "the fiercest attack of the enemy," which appears to correspond to Selden's early afternoon attack.

20. Alberts, *Rebels*, p. 44.

21. Meketa, *Legacy of Honor*, p. 167.

22. W. W. Mills, *Forty Years at El Paso* (El Paso: Carl Herzog, 1962).

23. E. O. Porter. "Letters Home: W. W. Mills Writes to his Family," *Password* 17 (Summer 1972), p. 81. Mills's estimates of Confederate strength do not correlate with the present assessment.

24. Alberts, *Rebels*, pp. 43–44.

25. Ibid., p. 44.

26. Simmons, *Albuquerque*, p. 161, and compiled service record of James Hubbell (Compiled Service Records of the Fourth and Fifth New Mexico Volunteers, RG 94, M427, Roll 40, NA).

Chapter 7

1. OR, I: 9, p. 519. Although several sources imply that the lancer charge occurred at about 3:00 P.M., Plympton and Robinson are quite

clear that it happened before Canby arrived (Plympton letter to Selden, dated February 24, 1862. Records of U. S. Continental Commands, 1821–1921, p. 1, entry 3183, RG 393, NA). Therefore, I assume that it took place between 2:00 and 2:30.

2. As high-ranking an officer as General Henry Halleck noted that "In a regular charge in line the lance offers great advantage." (Quoted in McWhiney, *Attack and Die*, p. 64). Jerry Thompson located one of the Confederate cavalry's guidon banners at a Texas auction and described it to the author.

3. Wayne Austerman, "Ancient Weapons in Modern War," *Civil War Times Illustrated* (March 1985), p. 23; Richard D. Steuart, "Cold Steel for the Yanks," *Confederate Veteran 35* (February 1927), pp. 50–52; Bennett H. Young, "Texas Cavalry Expedition in 1861–1862," *Confederate Veteran 21* (March 1913).

4. Austerman, "Ancient Weapons," p. 23.

5. Peticolas says that the order to charge was countermanded (Alberts, *Rebels*, pp. 53–54). However, note that Green does not discuss countermanding the order in his report (OR, I: 9, p. 519).

6. Ickis reports that Texans later told him that they mistook the Colorado Volunteers for New Mexican "Greasers" (Mumey, *Bloody Trails*, pp. 31, 76).

7. The use of a hollow-square formation by Dodd is noted by Whitford, in *Colorado Volunteers in the Civil War* (Glorieta: Rio Grande Press, 1989), p. 64 and is suggested by the square formation noted on Canby's battle map in the National Archives. While some have questioned whether this really happened, it was a recommended formation for infantry when dealing with cavalry attacks, and so it is credible that Dodd would have used it. Since it was normally a battalion maneuver with one company occupying each side of the square, Dodd probably directed each of the four sections of his single company to form a side of the square. See also Griffith, *Battle Tactics*, pp.

99–101, and Lippincott, *U.S. Infantry Tactics*, pp. 348–80.

8. Mumey, *Bloody Trails*, p. 76.

9. Ibid.

10. I have assumed that all twenty of the casualties in Lang's lancer company (B of the Fifth) occurred during this charge.

11. There were probably several slaves who accompanied their owners into New Mexico. Many of the Texans, including Green, Lang, and a private named John Wafford, are known to have had slaves with them. Undoubtedly there were others. Martin H. Hall "Negroes with Confederate Troops in West Texas and New Mexico," *Password 13* (Spring 1968).

12. Mumey, *Bloody Trails*, p. 86.

13. Plympton letter to Selden, though Ickis suggests that three of his colleagues were wounded (Mumey, *Bloody Trails*, p. 32).

14. Steuart, "Cold Steel," p. 51. Austerman, "Ancient Weapons," pp. 23–25.

15. Mumey, *Bloody Trails*, pp. 32, 76. Alberts, *Rebels*, p. 44.

16. Plympton letter.

17. Canby (OR, I: 9, p. 490) described the casualties in the morning's engagements as sixty-three wounded and ten killed. Collins (March 1, 1862) says that the losses prior to 1:00 P.M. were only twenty, but this seems low and may refer only to losses in Duncan's command. Chacón (Meketa, *Legacy of Honor*, p. 171) describes the transport of the wounded from the battlefield in "barrows."

18. Hall, *Confederate Army*, p. 46; Noel, *Campaign*, p. 20.

19. Sometime between the early afternoon crossing of the batteries and the late afternoon engagements, one of Hall's twenty-four-pounders was apparently disabled, since both Duncan and Carson refer to a single twenty-four-pounder in their reports of the afternoon's events. Evans, in his "Battles and Leaders" article, states that the howitzer had suffered a broken trail (the tailpiece on the cannon), making it impossible to move or to aim reliably.

In his report, Canby notes the recovery of a disabled gun during the retreat. Unfortunately, no one describes the circumstances surrounding the loss of the howitzer. Note that the Peticolas sketch (page 66) shows two Federal cannons facing the Confederate left. These are almost certainly Hall's twenty-four-pounders.

20. OR, I: 9, p. 490.

21. The location of McRae's battery can be inferred from the testimony of First Sergeant John Walker (Company D, First U.S. Cavalry) and Second Lieutenant W. T. Pennock (also of the First Cavalry) at Captain R. S. C. Lord's Court of Inquiry. (Ruhlen Collection, New Mexico State University.)

22. Collins (March 1, 1862) describes the initial disposition of Canby's left and Ickis (Mumey, *Bloody Trails*, p. 76) adds some additional detail. I have inferred that the troops were behind the riverbank before the Texan charge, based on the testimony at the Lord Court of Inquiry and Robinson's account ("Narrative of Events Pertaining to C and F Companies of the Seventh Infantry," Daniel Robinson Collection, Fort Laramie National Historical Site).

23. Estimated mid-afternoon Federal deployment at the ford:

Canby (Federal Left)

Headquarters	20 (assumed)
Colorado	70
McRae's Battery	90
Battery Support (Plympton)	
Mortimore	50
Hubbell	70
A, H/10	100
C,F,H/7	230
	630
Reserve	
Pino	590
Claflin	130
Lord	
	720

Center (Roberts)

Selden/Wingate	260
Carson	510
	770

Union Right (Duncan)

Duncan	210
Valdez	230
Brotherton	80
Barrientos	60
Hall	50
	630

24. One participant in the battle, A. Mennet, later reported that Sibley remained in his ambulance near the battlefield (Twitchell, *Leading Facts*, p. 376, n. 300). Several officers, including Lieutenant Thomas Ochiltree, stoutly defended Sibley, saying that he was suffering from pneumonia, not drunkenness, at Valverde. In addition, Lieutenant Joseph Draper Sayers said that Sibley was in the saddle from daybreak to 1:30 P.M. on February 21 (Thompson, *Henry Hopkins Sibley*, p. 313). Thompson notes that these officers' futures were closely tied to Sibley's and that their testimonials may reflect this.

25. These numbers are based on the listing in n. 9 of Chapter 6, modified to reflect the movement of Sutton and Jordan to the ford.

Chapter 8

1. Although Raguet says that the artillery piece on the left was assigned to Lieutenant Wood, Teel states that it was Reily's and that Wood was on the right (OR, I: 9, pp. 517, 524).

2. Alberts, *Rebels*, p. 46. Ochiltree was the son of the renown Virginia orator, Judge William P. Ochiltree (*National Cyclopedia*, vol. 2, p. 192).

3. Roe recalled that the twelve-pounders were on the right and the six-pounders and

mountain howitzer were on the left. Roe, "Recitals and Reminiscences."

4. Plympton letter. Note that, as discussed in n. 9 below, the Confederate fire was almost certainly canister, not grape.

5. OR, I: 9, p. 517.

6. Raguet's battalion included D/5, B/4, E/4, G/4, and H/4.

7. Meketa, *Legacy of Honor*, p. 168.

8. I infer that the train was reasonably close to the battlefield in the late afternoon because Shannon is reported to have arrived at McRae's battery shortly after it was overrun (OR, I: 9, p. 515) and because Raguet was concerned about the immediate loss of the train should the Union right have advanced (OR, I: 9, p. 517).

9. Yeary, *Reminiscences*, p. 577. It is almost certain that the Federal artillerymen did not use grapeshot, since an 1862 ammunition inventory shows no such rounds (see Wallen ammunition report) and since grapeshot was almost exclusively used by the navy in its large bore guns. It is far more likely that canister or shell was mistaken for grape. Evans also suggests that the Federals had no grapeshot in their ammunition chests (Evans, "Canby at Valverde").

10. Duncan says that he requested the assistance before Raguet's charge because he had been informed of "a concentrated movement of our whole left flank against the enemy's right" (OR, I: 9, p. 498). This is inconsistent with both Canby's stated strategy and his report, which says that he dispatched Ingraham, Wingate, and Carson in response to "urgent and repeated requests" from Duncan *after* Raguet's intent had begun to show itself (OR, I: 9, p. 490). Although it is plausible that the conservative Duncan really wanted additional troops to carry out the enfilading attack on the right wing (and simply transposed "left" and "right" in his report), I am inclined to believe Canby's account as regards the timing of Ingraham's move to the right wing.

11. Alberts, *Rebels*, p. 46.

12. Yeary, *Reminiscences*, pp. 612–13.

13. Canby says that the Confederates lost three guns during the battle (OR, I: 9, pp. 487–93). However, this is not confirmed in any Confederate reports or in any other Union reports.

14. Bell, "Campaign of New Mexico," p. 63, and Collins March 1, 1862.

15. Stewart, *Picket's Charge*, p. 67. See also McWhiney, *Attack and Die*, pp. 112–25.

16. Collins, March 1, 1862.

17. Scott letter. Although it would not have been unusual for a commander to encourage his troops before a charge, Green is unlikely to have said, "Follow me," since he would have been behind the charge rather than in front.

18. Alberts, *Rebels*, p. 48.

Chapter 9

General note: While the times from 4:00 P.M. to 5:00 P.M. have been estimated, they are consistent with the tenor of the official reports and the actions reported therein.

1. Michael Tate, "A Johnny Reb in Sibley's New Mexico Campaign: Reminiscences of Private Henry C. Wright," *East Texas Historical Review* 25 (1987), p. 27.

2. According to Stewart (Stewart, *Picket's Charge*, p. 118), the "ordinary rapid fire rate was about 2 rounds per minute to allow for reloading, repositioning, and re-aiming the cannons." He further notes, however, that in "an emergency" (for example, firing canister at close range with no need for aiming), the rate of fire could be as high as four rounds per minute. Ideally, riflemen could shoot three rounds per minute, but this was certainly an upper limit (see also Griffith, *Battle Tactics*, p. 207, n. 38).

3. Bell, "Campaign of New Mexico," p. 63.

4. Griffith, *Battle Tactics*, p. 99.

5. Evans ("Canby at Valverde") opines that McRae used "only round shot and spherical case; there was no grape."

6. Yeary, *Reminiscences*, pp. 6–7; Hall,

Confederate Army, pp. 99–100.

7. Griffith, *Battle Tactics*, p. 141 and McWhiney, *Attack and Die*, p. 42.

8. Ibid., p. 143.

9. There has been much controversy over the behavior of the New Mexico Volunteers at Valverde, especially their behavior during the defense of the battery. Some have said that all of them ran at the first hint of a Confederate attack, while others have suggested that they behaved no worse than the regulars. Having read all the sources, I conclude that the best reconstruction is as follows: a collapse of Mortimore's men on the left, infecting some or all of the men of the Tenth U.S. Infantry (and perhaps Company C of the Seventh) who retreated before the close-range and hand-to-hand fighting occurred. This is consistent with the casualty rates for these companies, the presumed location of Teel's battery on the far right of Scurry's forces, and the location of Plympton's men to the left rear of the battery. However, as discussed later, I believe that most or all of Hubbell's company moved to the battery and fought alongside the remaining regulars.

10. Plympton's letter, although clearly self-serving in this regard, describes the defense of the battery. There is no question that Hubbell's men did move forward to the battery since Roberts's testimony at the Lord Court of Inquiry describes them as "running to the rear" only after Wingate had arrived and the battery largely had been overrun.

11. Meketa estimates that there were 550 men in the defending force (Meketa, *Legacy of Honor*, p. 378, n. 12); a summation of units suggests that the number may have been as high as 610, at least initially, although some of the units may have been depleted by casualties. Canby notes that "the main body of his [Plympton's] command rushed the battery and engaged in a gallant and desperate attempt to repel the enemy" (OR, I: 9, p. 491). See also Mumey, *Bloody Trails*, p. 77.

12. I infer Hubbell's location on the right of the battery from Roberts's testimony. He notes that Hubbell's men were in front of Lord's position before he charged. Bascom's infamous exploits in pursuit of Cochise are detailed by Edwin Sweeney, in *Cochise—Chiricahua Apache Chief* (Norman: University of Oklahoma Press, 1993).

13. Collins, March 1, 1862.

14. Ibid. The sharpshooters in the trees are also mentioned by Stanley (*Fort Craig*, pp. 66–67) and by Hall (*Sibley's New Mexico Campaign*, p. 96). Collins is clearly incorrect when he asserts that all the gunners were killed—see n. 15 below.

15. In Porter, "W. W. Mills Letters," March 6, 1862, Mills estimated sixty casualties at McRae's battery. Canby's numbers give at most fifteen killed, twenty-three wounded, and two missing for a total of forty, even assuming that all of the casualties for the Third Cavalry occurred at the battery. Whitford (*Colorado Volunteers*, p. 65) says that fifteen of the ninety-three men working the guns were killed or seriously wounded. A careful compilation from post-battle records suggests that McRae lost nineteen killed, twenty-four wounded, and two missing for a total of forty-five casualties. While not as catastrophic as suggested by Mills, this is still a loss rate of over 50 percent. There is some question about whether or not Bell himself was wounded. At various times he reported wounds in his foot, in his chest, and a loss of hearing. However, his name does not appear on the official lists of wounded, and his pension claim in that regard was denied (information on Lieutenant Bell's pension request courtesy Charles Meketa).

16. Hall, *Confederate Army*, p. 219.

17. Alberts, *Rebels*, p. 48.

18. Mumey, *Bloody Trails*, p. 78; Alberts, *Rebels*, p. 48.

19. OR, I: 9, p. 638.

20. OR, I: 9, p. 522.

21. Porter, "W. W. Mills Letters," March 6, 1862.

22. Whitford, *Colorado Volunteers*, p. 65.

23. Roe, "Recitals and Reminiscences."

24. This is reported in "Guns of Valverde" (McMasters and Ruhlen, p. 22), Pettis ("Confederate Invasion," p. 108), and Whitford (*Colorado Volunteers*, p. 65). It adds a romantic touch, but is probably not true.

25. I infer that Wingate was wounded at this point because Canby refers to the four companies of the Fifth Infantry as "Wingate's Battalion" to this point and as "Selden's Battalion" from here on (OR, I: 9, p. 491). This is confirmed by Robinson's account.

26. Pino's official after-action report states that, far from fleeing in disarray as reported, he was "ordered back to form on the western bank" (OR, I: 9, p. 503). It is worth noting that this report went unchallenged (at least in the sense that Roberts challenged Duncan's report), despite Canby's allegation of Pino's unwillingness to reinforce the battery (OR, I: 9, p. 491).

27. Daniel Robinson Collection, p. 20.

28. Chacón says that Canby had three horses shot out from under him during the battle, but that seems inordinately high and is not otherwise reported, even by Canby's apologists. Mills (*Forty Years at El Paso*, p. 61) notes Canby's loss of his horse and his retrieval of the musket.

29. Daniel Robinson Collection, p. 20. There is some question about how effectively the Confederates were able to use McRae's cannons against the retreating Federals. It has been suggested (Meketa, *Legacy of Honor*, p. 379, n. 13) that because the Texas gunners were unable to aim the guns accurately, they were ineffective. In addition, it has been suggested that there was no ammunition available because the Union artillerymen had fired the limber boxes and caissons. In "Canby at Valverde" (p. 700), Evans also suggests that McRae's guns may have been "elevated for distant firing," and in their haste, the Texans failed to make the necessary adjustments to fire effectively at the retreating Federals. (This seems unlikely, given the close range of the fighting. However, some of the guns may have been "de-manned" early in the charge by the sharpshooters.) However, the Texas reports suggest that they were used effectively (OR, I: 9, p. 515). I am inclined to discount the Texan accounts. Alberts placed the total casualties during the retreat at twelve killed and twelve wounded, roughly 10 percent of the total Union casualties (Alberts, *Rebels*, p. 51n). However, he has subsequently stated that, based upon Meketa's casualty analysis, this number may be low.

30. Yeary, *Reminiscences*, pp. 760–61.

31. Alberts, *Rebels*, p. 48.

32. OR, I: 9, p. 491.

33. Gracy, "New Mexico Campaign Letters," p. 175; OR, I: 9, pp. 516–18.

34. OR, II: 53, p. 452.

Chapter 10

1. See Appendix, especially section entitled "A Qualitative Evaluation of Union Casualties."

2. Thompson, *Westward the Texans*, p. 89.

3. Sibley suggests that the white flag was initially assumed to be an indication of surrender, and he obliquely suggests that this may have held up his advance on Fort Craig. Given the circumstances and his particular state of mind, this seems unlikely (OR, I: 9, p. 508).

4. Martin H. Hall, "An Appraisal of the 1862 New Mexico Campaign: A Confederate Officer's Letter to Nacogdoches," *New Mexico Historical Review 51* (1976), p. 332.

5. OR, I: 9, p. 508.

6. Alberts, *Rebels*, p. 51; Thompson, *Westward the Texans*, p. 89.

7. Thomas Collins, "A Texan's Account of the Battle of Valverde," *Panhandle Plains Historical Review 37* (1964), pp. 33–35.

8. Mumey, *Bloody Trails*, pp. 33–34. Note that the number of wounded does not include several who would subsequently die from their injury (for example, Wingate) since they are included in the "killed" category.

9. OR, I: 9, p. 647. Pulveris licii was a cough medicine and expectorant made of pulverized licorice leaves.

10. On p. 33, Ickis says that he was searching for one John McKee, whose body was found some six weeks later floating in the river. On p. 82, he says he was looking for Harrison Berry. Both men appear in his casualty list on p. 79. Ickis finally concludes that Berry has gone "up country," that is, deserted (Mumey, *Bloody Trails*, p. 83).

11. OR, I: 9, p. 487.

12. OR, I: 9, p. 633; Meketa, *Legacy of Honor*, p. 182.

13. OR, I: 9, p. 633.

14. Meketa, *Legacy of Honor*, p. 171.

15. Ibid., p. 174 (quoting a letter from John W. Ellis).

16. Mumey, *Bloody Trails*, p. 82.

17. See Chapter 2, n. 13.

18. Stanley, *Civil War*. Marion Grinstead related to the author that in the 1970s she talked with an elderly farmer named Vigil from the now-abandoned village of Clyde, which had been established at the site of the village of Valverde (Marshall and Walt, *Rio Abajo*, p. 287). According to Mr. Vigil, farmers who planted in the area between the village and Mesa del Contadero would occasionally plow up skulls and other human bones when they prepared their fields for spring planting.

19. Hall, *Confederate Army*, p. 219.

20. Letter from H. J. Hunter to Jettie Word dated April 4, 1862 (courtesy Jerry Thompson).

21. Thompson, *Westward the Texans*, p. 89; Mumey, *Bloody Trails*, p. 82.

22. Gracy, "New Mexico Campaign Letters," p. 175.

23. OR, I: 9, p. 632.

24. Meketa, *Legacy of Honor*, pp. 170–71; Daniel Robinson Collection, p. 20.

25. OR, II: 53, pp. 513–14.

26. Alberts, *Rebels*, p. 118.

27. Robert Kerby, *The Confederate Invasion of Arizona and New Mexico* (Tucson: Westernlore Press, 1981), p. 58.

28. Hall, "Appraisal," quoting Captain W. L. Alexander.

29. OR, II: 53, pp. 792–93.

30. James Richardson, *A Compilation of Messages and Papers of the Confederacy: 1861–1865* (Nashville: United States Publishing Company, 1905), vol. 1, p. 215, and vol. 6, p. 231.

31. The Barrientos affair is described in *Legacy of Honor* (Meketa, *Legacy of Honor*, p. 374, n. 4). Although Barrientos was found guilty of desertion, his men were exonerated since they were determined to have been following what they believed to be lawful orders.

32. Whitford, *Colorado Volunteers*, p. 68.

33. Connelly's concerns were apparently justified since he later reported that his home had been "despoiled of its earlier contents, including a valuable stock of food and everything in the way of subsistence" by the Texans (OR, I: 9, pp. 651–52).

34. Although he is not specific as to when he left, he states that he arrived in Santa Fe on the twenty-seventh. Considering the pressure of the situation and assuming a short stop in Los Pinos, a two-day trip seems to be a reasonable assumption.

35. Calvin Horn, *New Mexico's Troubled Years* (Albuquerque: Horn and Wallace, 1963), p. 101. Connelly actually moved the territorial offices to a hotel that he owned in Las Vegas.

36. In fact, Canby's initial report on the casualties suffered by the Colorado Volunteers showed two dead, twenty-eight wounded, and nine missing from a cadre of seventy-one men (OR, I: 9, p. 493).

Chapter 11

1. Alberts, *Rebels*, p. 52.

2. The confiscation of material from Stapleton's store is described by both Peticolas (Alberts, *Rebels*, p. 52) and Howell (Thompson, *Westward the Texans*, p. 89). Sibley was later accused of appropriating some of the confiscated material for his personal use. Thompson feels that this charge is probably false (Thompson, *Henry Hopkins Sibley*, p. 312, and Thompson, *Westward the Texans*, p. 152, n. 79).

3. Jerry Thompson has determined that this hospital was located in the Dionisio Jaramillo residence on the village plaza.

4. The mass slaughter of the mules at Johnson's Ranch, reported in early chronicles of the Battle of Glorieta, is still debated. A recent article by Leo Oliva, "Chivington and the Mules at Johnson's Ranch," *Wagon Tracks 6* (August 1992), suggests that most of the mules were probably run off and that only thirty or so were actually killed by Chivington and his men.

5. For a thoughtful summary of the engagement at Glorieta, see Thomas Edrington, "The Confederate Victory at Pigeon's Ranch," published by General William R. Scurry Camp—Sons of Confederate Veterans, 1987.

6. OR, I: 9, p. 512.

7. OR, I: 9, pp. 511–12.

8. Immediately after the capture of the battery at Valverde, Captain Sayers was given command of the six captured cannons. The unit persisted for the duration of the war, although McRae's original guns were gradually replaced by more capable weapons (McMasters and Ruhlen, "Guns of Valverde").

9. Colonel James Reily article in the San Antonio *Herald*, July 12, 1862 (courtesy Jerry Thompson).

10. Jeff Riddle, *The Indian History of the Modoc War* (San Jose: Urion Press, 1914), chapter 10.

11. Don Thrapp, *Encyclopedia of Frontier Biography* (Glendale: Arthur H. Clark Co., 1988); Stanley reports (incorrectly) that Duncan was the patron of the Duncan Opera House in Las Vegas, New Mexico, after the war (Stanley, *Civil War*, p. 246).

12. There were two Fort Wingates—one established in 1862 near present-day San Rafael, New Mexico, and one established in 1860 near present-day Gallup. The latter post was originally named Fort Fauntleroy, until its namesake, Colonel Thomas J. Fauntleroy, resigned to join the Confederacy. The post was renamed Fort Lyon in August 1861. This post was abandoned in September 1861 and reoccupied in 1868. The original Fort Wingate was abandoned in June 1868 and the garrison was relocated to Fort Lyon. The combined post was then renamed Fort Wingate. Robert Frazer, *Forts of the West* (Norman: University of Oklahoma Press, 1965), pp. 108–9.

13. United States Military Academy Association of Graduates, *Forty-Sixth Annual Reunion of the Association of Graduates of the United States Military Academy* (Saginaw: Seeman and Peters, 1915), pp. 142–47.

14. A canyon on the eastern bank of Elephant Butte Reservoir and a street in El Paso, Texas, were also named in McRae's honor.

15. Heyman, *Prudent Soldier*, pp. 191, 225.

16. Texas had attempted to "invade" New Mexico on at least two previous occasions. In 1841, an expedition ostensibly to establish trade was overwhelmed by Mexican forces and dragged to prison in Mexico City. The troops experienced not only the depredations of the long march in chains, but also executions, torture, and starvation before being repatriated in 1842. Again in 1843, a group of Texans was stopped and disarmed by U.S. troops in the Texas panhandle on their way to Santa Fe (Joe Frantz, "An End to the Beginning," *Texas Highways* [May 1986], pp. 30–37).

17. Note that the overall casualties include missing, which may include some desertions from Mortimore's company.

18. Morale may have been an issue since it was Pino's command that cowered under Teel's cannonade the previous afternoon and that had been subjected to "stern measures" in Belen the previous month, when they "rioted" to protest their lack of clothing and pay.

19. OR, I: 9, pp. 492, 638.

20. OR, I: 9, pp. 638.

21. Collins, March 1, 1862; Plympton letter.

22. The details of the Court of Inquiry proceedings clearly vindicate Lord. His gallantry at Gettysburg is described in Stanley (*Fort Craig*, p. 66) and McWhiney (*Attack and Die*, p. 138).

23. Mumey, *Bloody Trails*, p. 67. Note that Rossell was paroled by the Texans almost immediately and was injured in an explosion a few days later on a road-building assignment near Hatch's Ranch, New Mexico.

24. Per Francis Heitman, in *Historical Record and Dictionary of the United States Army* (repr., 1903; Urbana: University of Illinois Press, 1965), the following Union brevet promotions occurred as a direct result of the Battle of Valverde:

> David Brotherton to major
> Ira Claflin to captain
> George Howland to major
> Robert Morris to major
> Benjamin Roberts to colonel
> George Rossell to major
> Joseph Tilford to major
> Benjamin Wingate to major

25. Francis Kennedy, *Civil War Battlefield Guide* (Boston: Houghton Mifflin Company, 1990), p. 301; and Newton Strait, *An Alphabetical List of Battles* (U.S. Department of the Interior, Bureau of Pensions, 1905).

Appendix

1. Hall, *Confederate Army*.

2. OR, I: 9, pp. 630–31.

3. Compiled Service Records of the First Regiment of New Mexico Volunteers, RG 94, M427, rolls 1–34, NA. Compiled Service Records of the First New Mexico Militia, RG 94, M427, roll 35, NA. Compiled Service Records of the Second New Mexico Volunteers, RG 94, M427, rolls 36–37, NA. Compiled Service Records of the Third New Mexico Volunteers, RG 94, M427, rolls 38–39, NA. Compiled Service Records of the Fourth and Fifth New Mexico Volunteers, RG 94, M427, roll 40, NA. Miscellaneous Service Records—New Mexico, RG 94, M427, rolls 44–46, NA. Index to Compiled Service Records of the Colorado Volunteers, RG 94, M534, rolls 1–3.

4. Fort Craig post returns (Returns from U.S. Military Posts, RG 94, M617, roll 261, NA) suggest that the two companies of the First Cavalry totaled 133. However, Nicodemus lists only Company D (with the HQ) and does not even show Company G (OR, I: 9, pp. 630–31). I have set them approximately equal to one another.

5. This includes Duncan and his staff. Roberts and his staff are probably included with the overall HQ.

6. Nicodemus shows Wingate's battalion (B/5, D/5, F/5, I/5) at 306 (OR, I, 9: pp. 630–31). The post returns suggest 259.

7. Nicodemus shows Plympton's battalion (C/7, F/7, A/10, H/10, CO) at 310 (OR, I: 9, pp. 630–31). The post returns have 334.

8. Nicodemus shows Hall's battery (F/10) as thirty-seven, whereas the post returns have forty-eight (OR, I: 9, pp. 630–31).

9. Nicodemus shows McRae at 130 (OR, I: 9, pp. 630–31). The post returns show 85. Anecdotal battle reports suggest as many as 95.

10. Ickis says that only seventy-one Coloradans participated in the battle (Mumey, *Bloody*

Trails, p. 76). The post returns suggest eighty-four.

11. According to Nicodemus, Colonel Miguel Pino's Fourth column included four companies of the Second New Mexico Volunteers under Lieutenant Colonel Chavez and two companies each of the Second and Third New Mexico volunteers under Major Pino (OR, I: 9, pp. 630–31). The records of the Second New Mexico Volunteers are unclear, but suggestive of participation by seven companies rather than six (A, B, C, D, F, H, and I).

12. I have assumed that Companies F and L of the Third New Mexico Volunteers, which are not mentioned otherwise, constituted roughly half of the Second Battalion of Pino's Fourth column as listed by Nicodemus.

13. By a process of elimination using service-record entries, I hypothesize that Companies H and K were detailed to the fort during the battle. Neither of these companies is specifically mentioned in the reports, neither had any battle casualties (although both had some desertions on the day of the battle), and no service-record entries indicate battle involvement (for example, no horses killed or equipment lost). The other companies all have some direct or indirect indication of battlefield involvement.

14. Nicodemus does not show Graydon at all (OR, I: 9, pp. 630–31).

15. Nicodemus's letter of February 16 shows 272 militiamen in Canby's Fifth column and 200 New Mexico Mounted Militia in his Second column (OR, I: 9, pp. 630–31). However, this may not include the six companies of militia that arrived on the nineteenth and twentieth. Canby says that he had "about 1,000 hastily collected and unorganized militia," but this may include some of the volunteers whom he held in rather low regard. By tallying up the other forces and assuming that Canby's estimate of 3,801 troops is accurate, I conclude that there were about 520 militiamen at the fort.

16. Thompson, *Westward the Texans*, p. 89.

17. Alberts, *Rebels*, p. 49.

18. The February Post Return from Fort Craig also lists Henry Schweeb as killed and C. J. Baum, Theodore Bridges, John Hoey, I. T. Newman, Samuel Rintlin, Samuel Simonson, and S. W. T. Young as wounded. However, there are no service records showing these men as members of the Colorado Volunteers in the U.S. National Archives.

19. Alleged deserters from the Second New Mexico Volunteers (spelled per service record entries):

Company A (28)

Pablo Analla, José Andrada, José María Gonzales, Polinario Lovato, Faustin Lujan, Marcelino Martin, Roman Martin, Vicente Martin, Florentino Medrano, José Medrano, Margarito Montoya, Guadalupe Ortega, José María Ortega, Herculino Ortiz, Juan de Jesús Padilla, Juan José Pena, Merced Perales, Antonio José Pineda, Marcus Rael, Bencisla Rivera, Manuel Rivera, Francisco Rodriguez, Pablo Romero, Nasario Salazar, Anase Sandoval, Margarito Servantes, Dioisio Urban, Leandro Varela.

Company B (14)

Emilio Abeita, Jesús García, Rafael Herrera, Pedro Maes, Encarnacio Martin, José Ygnacio Martin, José Manuel Martin, José María Maestas, Francisco Padilla, Jesús Robles, Alejandro Romero, Dilubino Romero, Juan Samora, Felix Vasquez.

Company C (15)

José Ignacio Abeytia, Rufigio Acosta, Casildo Baca, Jesús Duran, Nicholas Gallegos, Antonio Gonzales, Gregorio Gonzales, José Antonio Lucero, Juan Felipe Martin, Juan Bisente Montano, José Francisco Montoya, José Ignacio Montoya, Ambrocio Moreno, Gabriel Olaga, Manuel Antonio Valencia.

Company D (15)

Dolores Analla, Cristoval Archuleta, Juan Benavides, José Candelaria, Jacinto Gallegos, Manuel Gonzales, Mateo Gonzalez, Dolores Martin, Manuel Martin, Juan Marta Miera, Rumaldo Montoya, Juan Ocana, Juan Ortega, Juan Antonio Sanches, Damacio Tafolla.

Company F (3)

Estanislado Acosta, Salamon Caravajal, Luis Romero.

Company G

None

Company H (24)

Francisco Alderete, Juan Baca, Ambrosio Belasques, Juan Andres Bustamante, Candido Chaves, Juan Gallego Chaves, Juan Coronodo, Jesús María Gonsales, Marselo Griego, Juan Lobato, Julio Maes, Rafael Montano, Ramón Montoya, José María Pena, José de Jesús Romero, Juan Sisneros, Olallo Taurin, Antonio Torres, Juan José Torres, Juan Pedro Torres, José Ramón Trujillo, Juan José Trujillo, Quilino Trujillo, Rafael Trujillo.

Company I (28)

Estanislado Acosta, Deonicio Acuna, Silvestro Alderete, Francisco Baca, Juan José Baca, Lorenzo Baca, Francisco Benabides, José María Benabides, Matias Bigil, Sabino Cadena, Juan de Jesús Duran, Relles Escarote, Dimas Flores, Alvino García, Bietor García, Francisco Gomez, Manuel Gonzales, Francisco Gonsales, Jesús Marques, Gregoria Pacheco, Ramón Padilla, Felipe Perea, Francisco Rael, Jesús Rameres, Francisco Sanchez, José Antonio Sanchez, Juan Tapia, Jesús Trujillo.

Company K (20?)[*]

Pablo Baca, Pedro Benavides, Pedro Carasco, José Manuel Chavez, Florencio Cordova, Victor Duran, Gregorio Espinosa, Juan Gabaldon, Camilio Lunro, Antonio Marques, Demetrio Mascarenes, José Saturnino Mascarenes, Casimera Mayo, Crispin Peralta, Felipe Peralta, Juan Peralta, Nicolas Romero, Leocadia Samora, Pedro Sisneros, Lino Tarrin.

20. Text of General Order no. 43, dated May 7, 1862:

> All deserters from the New Mexican Volunteers and Militia, except such as are under charges for mutiny, for joining the enemy, or for taking up arms against the Government, are hereby discharged from the service of the United States and will be pardoned if, within thirty days from the date of this order, they return to their homes, report themselves to the Alcaldes of their several precincts, and resume their customary vocations.
>
> The Alcaldes throughout the Territory will, at the expiration of the thirty days specified above, report to this office through the Prefects of their Districts, the name, Company, and regiment of every deserter from the Volunteers or Militia, who may have reported to them and in good faith have resumed his former occupation.
>
> All who fail to avail themselves of this conditional pardon will be regarded and treated as deserters, whenever and wherever they may be found, and no

---

[*] There is some question whether or not Company K was at Valverde. The men listed were granted amnesty under General Order 43 in May 1862.

deserter from these troops will be allowed again to enter the service of the United States.

It is represented that many of the deserters have organized themselves into bands of robbers and infest the country in the neighborhood of Cuvero [*sic*], Manzana [*sic*], Chillili [*sic*], Tijeras, San Antonio, and San Francisco, subsisting themselves by plundering the inhabitants of the neighboring country. These bands will be suppressed and upon conviction and sentence by military commissions, the members will be summarily punished as marauders and highway robbers; and whoever may harbor or protect these outlaws, purchase their plunder, aid them in concealing it, or in any other manner whatsoever render them assistance will be treated as principals.

By order of Col. E. R. S. Canby
Gordon Chapin
Acting Army Adjutant General

21. Miller, "Hispanos," p. 114.

Bibliography

Manuscript Sources

Daniel Robinson Collection, Fort Laramie
National Historical Site, U. S. National
Park Service

National Archives of the United States
Record Group 75: Letters Received by
the Office of Indian Affairs.
Record Group 94, M617: Returns
from U.S. Military Posts.
Record Group 94, M427: Compiled
Service Records of the New
Mexico Volunteers.
Record Group 94, M534: Index to
Compiled Service Records of the
Colorado Volunteers.
Record Group 393: Records of U. S.
Continental Commands, 1821–
1921, pt I.

Texas State Archives

Ruhlen Collection, New Mexico State University

Government Documents

General Services Administration—National
Archives and Record Service. "Military
Operations of the Civil War—Volume IV,"
1980.

Gideon, J. S. *Cavalry Tactics—First Part*. U.S.
War Department, Washington, D.C.,
1841.

Proceedings of a Court of Inquiry in the Case of
Captain R. S. C. Lord, First U.S. Cavalry
by Headquarters, Department of New
Mexico under Special Order No. 171,
September 22, 1862.

Robinson, T. W. "Introduction, Spread, and
Areal Extent of Saltcedar (Tamarix) in the
Western States." U.S. Geological Survey
Professional Paper 491A, 1965.

Strait, Newton A. *An Alphabetical List of Battles:
1754–1900*. U.S. Department of the
Interior, Bureau of Pensions, 1905.

United States Army. *Official Army Register of the
Volunteer Forces of the United States Army,
1861–1865*, pt. 8, 1867.

———. Military Division of the Missouri.
*Outline Descriptions of the Posts in the
Military Division of the Missouri*. Chicago,
1876.

United States Geophysical Survey. "Fort Craig,
New Mexico Quadrangle." 7.5 Minute
Topographic Map Series.

———. "Paraje Well, New Mexico Quadrangle." 7.5 Minute Topographic Map
Series.

———. "Pope, New Mexico Quadrangle." 7.5
Minute Topographic Map Series.

———. "San Marcial, New Mexico Quadrangle." 7.5 Minute Topographic Map
Series.

———. "Val Verde, New Mexico Quadrangle."
15 Minute Topographic Map Series.

———. "Oscura Mountains, New Mexico." 30 x
60 Minute Topographic Map Series.

United States Government Printing Office.
"Report of the Joint Committee on the
Conduct of the War." Senate Document
no. 108, 37th Cong., 3d sess., vol. 3,
364–72 (Invasion of New Mexico), 1863.

———. *The War of the Rebellion: A Compilation of the Official Records of the Union and Confederate Armies*, 128 vols. Washington, D. C., 1880–1901.

———. *United States Army Regulations of 1861*, rev. 1863 ed. Yuma: Fort Yuma Press, 1980.

Diaries and Journals

Alberts, Don, ed. *Rebels on the Rio Grande: The Civil War Journal of A. B. Peticolas.* Albuquerque: University of New Mexico Press, 1984.

Anderson, Hattie M. "With the Confederates in New Mexico—Memoirs of Hank Smith." *Panhandle Plains Historical Review* 2 (1929), 65–97.

Faulkner, W. A. "With Sibley in New Mexico: The Journal of William Henry Smith." *West Texas Historical Association Yearbook* 27 (October 1951), 111–42.

Gracy, David B., ed. "New Mexico Campaign Letters of Frank Starr—1861–1862." *Texas Military History* 4 (Fall 1964), 169–88.

Hanna, Ebenezer. *Journal of Ebenezer Hanna.* Texas State Archives.

Mumey, Nolie. *Bloody Trails along the Rio Grande—A Day-by-Day Diary of Alonzo Ferdinand Ickis.* Denver: The Old West Publishing Company, 1958.

Thompson, Jerry D., ed. *Westward the Texans: The Civil War Journal of Private William Randolph Howell.* El Paso: Texas Western Press, 1990.

Newspapers

Albuquerque Journal
Albuquerque Tribune
Galveston Weekly News
National Tribune
San Antonio Herald
Santa Fe Gazette

Personal communication

Steven Dupree
Charles and Jacqueline Meketa

Lee Myers
Jerry D. Thompson

Dissertations and Theses

Boyd, Douglas K. *Paraje de Fra Cristobal: Investigations of a Territorial Period Hispanic Village Site in Southern New Mexico.* Amarillo: U.S. Department of the Interior, Bureau of Reclamation, Southwest Region, May 1986.

Jamieson, Perry D. "The Development of Civil War Tactics." Ph.D. Diss., Wayne State University, 1979.

Books

Coates, Earl J., and Dean S. Thomas. *An Introduction to Civil War Small Arms.* Gettysburg: Thomas Publications, 1990.

Cohrs, Timothy, and Thomas J. Caperton. *Fort Selden, New Mexico.* Santa Fe: Museum of New Mexico Press, 1974.

Colton, Ray C. *The Civil War in the Western Territories.* Norman: University of Oklahoma Press, 1959.

Conner, Seymour, and Jimmy Skaggs. *Broadcloth and Britches—The Santa Fe Trade.* College Station: Texas A&M Press, 1977.

Dictionary of American Biography. New York: Charles Scribner's Sons, 1990.

Dornbusch, C. E. *Military Bibliography of the Civil War, vol. 2.* New York: New York Public Library, 1971.

Estergreen, M. Morgan. *Kit Carson—A Portrait in Courage.* Norman: University of Oklahoma Press, 1962.

Faulk, Odie. *General Tom Green—Fightin' Texan.* Waco: Texian Press, 1963.

Foote, Shelby. *The Civil War*, 3 vols. New York: Vintage Books, 1986.

Frazer, Robert W. *Forts of the West.* Norman: University of Oklahoma Press, 1965.

Ganaway, Loomis M. *New Mexico and the Sectional Controversy.* Albuquerque: University of New Mexico Press, 1944.

Gregg, Andrew K. *New Mexico in the Nineteenth Century—A Pictorial History.* Albuquerque: University of New Mexico Press, 1968.

———. *Drums of Yesterday: The Forts of New Mexico*. San Francisco: The Press of the Territories, 1968.

Griffith, Paddy. *Battle Tactics of the Civil War*. New Haven: Yale University Press, 1987.

Grinstead, Marion C. *Life and Death of a Frontier Fort: Fort Craig, New Mexico, 1854–1885*. Socorro: Socorro County Historical Society, 1973.

———. *Destiny at Valverde: The Life and Death of Alexander McRae*. Socorro: Socorro Historical Society, 1992.

Hall, Martin H. *Sibley's New Mexico Campaign*. Austin: University of Texas Press, 1960.

———. *The Confederate Army of New Mexico*. Austin: Presidial Press, 1978.

Hardee, W. J. *Rifle and Light Infantry Tactics for the Exercise and Maneuvers of Troops when Acting as Light Infantry or Riflemen*. Philadelphia: Lippincott, Grambo and Company, 1855.

Heitman, Francis B. *Historical Record and Dictionary of the United States Army*. U.S. Government Printing Office, 1903. Repr., Urbana: University of Illinois Press, 1965.

Heyman, Max. *Prudent Soldier—A Biography of Major General E. R. S. Canby*. Glendale: Arthur H. Clark Publishers, 1959.

Hollister, Ovando. *Boldly They Rode*. Lakewood: The Golden Press, 1949.

Horgan, Paul. *Great River*. New York: Rinehart and Company, 1954.

Horn, Calvin. *New Mexico's Troubled Years*. Albuquerque: Horn and Wallace Publishers, 1963.

Horn and Wallace, publishers, ed. *Confederate Victories in the Southwest—Prelude to Defeat*. Albuquerque: Horn and Wallace, 1961.

Johnson, Robert U., and Clarence C. Buel, eds. *Battles and Leaders of the Civil War*, vol. 2, 1883. Repr., Secaucus: Castle Press, n.d.

Josephy, Alvin M. Jr., ed. *War on the Frontier—The Trans-Mississippi West*. Richmond: Time–Life Books, 1986.

———. *The Civil War in the American West*. New York: Alfred A. Knopf, 1991.

Keleher, W. A. *Turmoil in New Mexico: 1848–1868*. Santa Fe: Rydal Press, 1952.

Kennedy, Francis H., ed. *The Civil War Battlefield Guide*. Boston: Houghton Mifflin Company, 1990.

Kerby, Robert Lee. *The Confederate Invasion of New Mexico and Arizona*. Tucson: Westernlore Press, 1981.

Linderman, Gerald F. *Embattled Courage: The Experience of Combat in the American Civil War*. New York: The Free Press, 1987.

Lippincott, J. B. *U.S. Infantry Tactics for the Instruction, Exercise, and Maneuvers of the United States Infantry*. Philadelphia: J. B. Lippincott and Co., 1861.

Mahan, D. H. *An Elementary Treatise on Advanced-Guard, Outpost, and Detachment of Troops*. New York: John Wiley, 1861.

Marshall, Michael P., and Henry J. Walt. *Rio Abajo—Prehistory and History of a Rio Grande Province*. Santa Fe: New Mexico State Office of Historic Preservation, 1984.

McWhiney, Grady, and Perry D. Jamieson. *Attack and Die: Civil War Military Tactics and the Southern Heritage*. Tuscaloosa: The University of Alabama Press, 1982.

Meketa, Charles, and Jacqueline Meketa. *One Blanket and Ten Days Rations*. Globe: Southwest Parks and Monument Association, 1980.

Meketa, J. D. *Louis Felsenthal, Citizen Soldier of Territorial New Mexico*. Albuquerque: University of New Mexico Press, 1982.

———, ed. *Legacy of Honor—The Life of Rafael Chacón*. Albuquerque: University of New Mexico Press, 1986.

Mills, W. W. *Forty Years at El Paso*. El Paso: Carl Herzog, 1962.

National Cyclopedia of American Biography. New York: James T. White and Co., 1907.

Noel, Theophilus. *A Campaign from Santa Fe to the Mississippi—Being a History of the Old Sibley Brigade*, 1865. Repr., Raleigh: Whittet and Shepperson Press, 1961.

Oates, Stephen B. *Confederate Cavalry West of the River*. Austin: University of Texas Press, 1961.

Pearce, T. M. *New Mexico Place Names*. Albuquerque: University of New Mexico Press, 1965.

Quaile, Milo M., ed. *Kit Carson's Autobiography*. Chicago: The Lakeside Press, 1935.

Richardson, James D. *A Compilation of Messages and Papers of the Confederacy: 1861–1865*. Nashville: United States Publishing Company, 1905.

Riddle, Jeff C. *The Indian History of the Modoc War*. San Jose: Urion Press, 1914.

Simmons, Marc. *Albuquerque*. Albuquerque: University of New Mexico Press, 1982.

Stanley, F. *The Civil War in New Mexico*. Denver: The World Press, 1960.

———. *Fort Craig*. Pampa: Pampa Print Shop, 1963.

Stewart, George R. *Picket's Charge—A Microhistory of the Final Charge at Gettysburg*. Boston: Houghton Mifflin Co., 1959.

Sweeney, Edwin. *Cochise—Chiricahua Apache Chief*. Norman: University of Oklahoma Press, 1993.

Thomas, Dean S. *Cannons—An Introduction to Civil War Artillery*. Gettysburg: Thomas Publications, 1985.

Thompson, Jerry D. *Henry Hopkins Sibley, Confederate General of the West*. Natchitoches: Northwestern State University Press, 1987.

———. *Desert Tiger: Captain Paddy Graydon and the Civil War in the Far Southwest*. El Paso: Texas Western Press, 1992.

Thrapp, Don L. *Encyclopedia of Frontier Biography*. Glendale: Arthur H. Clark Co., 1988.

Twitchell, Ralph E. *Leading Facts of New Mexico History*, vol. 2. Cedar Rapids: The Torch Press, 1912.

United States Military Academy Association of Graduates. *Forty-Sixth Annual Reunion of the Association of Graduates of the United States Military Academy, June 11, 1915*. Saginaw: Seeman and Peters, 1915.

Wagner, Arthur L. *Organization and Tactics*. New York: Westerman and Company, 1895.

Warner, Ezra J. *Generals in Grey*. Baton Rouge: Louisiana State University Press, 1959.

———. *Generals in Blue*. Baton Rouge: Louisiana State University Press, 1964.

Whitford, W. C. *Colorado Volunteers in the Civil War*. Glorieta: Rio Grande Press, 1989.

Williams, Jerry L., ed. *New Mexico in Maps*. Albuquerque: University of New Mexico Press, 1986.

Woodhead, Henry, series director. *The Civil War*, 27 vols. Alexandria: Time–Life Books, 1985.

Yeary, Mamie, ed. *Reminiscences of the Boys in Grey*, 1912. Repr., Dayton: Morningside Press, 1986.

Articles

Alberts, Don. "The Corps of Engineers and New Mexico's Water." *New Mexico Historical Review* 51 (April 1976), 93–108.

———. "The Battle of Peralta." *New Mexico Historical Review* 58 (October 1983), 369–79.

Archambeau, Ernest R., Jr. "The New Mexico Campaign, 1861–1862." *Panhandle–Plains Historical Review* 37 (1964), 3–32.

Arneson, David. "Rio Grande—The Battle for Valverde, 1861–62." *Strategy and Tactics* 143 (June 1991), 5–17.

Austerman, Wayne. "Ancient Weapons in Modern War: The South's Legion of Lancers." *Civil War Times Illustrated* (March 1985) 20–25.

Bell, J. M. "The Campaign of New Mexico, 1862." In *War Papers Read before the Commandery of the State of Wisconsin Military Order of the Loyal Legion of the United States*, 47–71. Milwaukee: Burdick, Armitage, and Allen, 1891.

Browne, P. D. "Captain T. D. Nettles and the Valverde Battery." *Texana* 2 (Spring 1964), 1–23.

Bryan, Howard. "The Man Who Buried the Cannons." *New Mexico Magazine* (January 1962), 13–15.

Charleton, Russell C. "The Civil War Years." *New Mexico Magazine* (April 1962), 32.

Collins, Thomas Benton. "A Texan's Account of the Battle of Valverde." *Panhandle–Plains Historical Review* 37 (1964), 33–35.

Cook, George. "Letter from the Front." *New Mexico Magazine* (September 1965), 2–4.

Edwards, Harold. "Captain Saturnino Baca in the Shadow of the Lincoln County War." *Los Amigos.* Lincoln: Lincoln County Heritage Trust (April 1993).

Fireman, Bert M. "How Far Westward the Civil War." In *The 1963 All Posse Corral Brand Book of the Denver Posse of the Westerners,* ed. Robert C. Cormack, 164–70. Morrison, CO: Buffalo Bill Press, 1965.

Frantz, Joe B. "An End to the Beginning." *Texas Highways* (May 1986), 30–37.

Grinstead, Marion C. "Alexander McRae—A Soldier's Letters Home." *Password* 11 (Winter 1966), 157–61.

Hall, Martin H. "Colonel James Reily's Diplomatic Missions to Chihuahua and Sonora." *New Mexico Historical Review* 31 (1956), 232–42.

———. "Native Mexican Relations in Confederate Arizona: 1861–1862." *Journal of Arizona History* 8 (April 1967), 171–78.

———. "Negroes with Confederate Troops in West Texas and New Mexico." *Password* 13 (Spring 1968), 11–12.

———. "Planter vs. Frontiersman: Conflict in Confederate Indian Policy." In *Essays on the American Civil War,* ed. Frank E. Vandiver et al., 45–72. Austin: University of Texas Press, 1968.

———. "An Appraisal of the 1862 New Mexico Campaign: A Confederate Officer's Letter to Nacogdoches." *New Mexico Historical Review* 51 (1976), 329–35.

Long, E. B. "War Beyond the River—Our Civil War and the Uncivil West." In *The Denver Westerner's Brand Book,* ed. Alan J. Stewart, 93–118. Boulder, CO: Johnson Publishing Co., 1977.

McCoy, Raymond. "The Battle of Valverde," *New Mexico Magazine* (September 1952), 24.

———. "Confederate Cannon" *New Mexico Magazine* (September 1953), 18.

———. "Victory at Ft. Fillmore." *New Mexico Magazine* (August 1961), 20.

McMaster, Richard K., and George Ruhlen. "The Guns of Valverde." *Password* 5 (1960), 21–34.

Meketa, Charles, and Jacqueline Meketa. "Heroes or Cowards? A New Look at the Role of Native New Mexicans at the Battle of Valverde." *New Mexico Historical Review* 62 (January 1987), 33–46.

Melzer, Richard. "Floods Haven't Washed Away Memories of Railroad Town." *New Mexico Magazine* (July 1990), 86–92.

Miller, Darlis. "Hispanos and the Civil War in New Mexico—A Reconsideration." *New Mexico Historical Review* 54 (1979), 105–23.

Myers, Lee M. "New Mexico Volunteers: 1862–1866" *The Smoke Signal* 37 (1979), 138–51.

Oder, Broech N. "The New Mexico Campaign." *Civil War Times* (August 1978), 22–28.

Oliva, Leo E. "Chivington and the Mules at Johnson's Ranch." *Wagon Tracks—The Santa Fe Trail Association Quarterly* 6 (August 1992), 16–17.

Porter, E. O. "Letters Home: W. W. Mills Writes to his Family." *Password* 17 (Spring 1972), 5–22; 17 (Summer 1972), 74–83; 17 (Fall 1972), 116–33; 17 (Winter 1972), 177–90.

Steere, Edward. "Rio Grande Campaign Logistics." *Military Review* (November 1953), 20–33.

Steuart, Richard D. "Cold Steel for the Yanks." *Confederate Veteran* 35 (February 1927), 50–52.

Tate, Michael L., ed. "A Johnny Reb in Sibley's New Mexico Campaign: Reminiscences of Private Henry C. Wright, 1861–1862." *East Texas Historical Review* 25 (1987), 20–33.

Thompson, Jerry D. "Mexican–Americans in the Civil War: The Battle of Valverde." *Texana* 10 (1972), 1–19.

———. "The Vulture over the Carrion." *Journal of Arizona History* 24 (Winter 1983), 381–404.

———. "The Civil War Diary of Major Charles Emil Wesche." *Password* 39 (Spring 1994), 37–47.

Waldrip, William I. "New Mexico during the Civil War." *New Mexico Historical Review* 28 (July 1953), 163–291.

Walker, Charles. "Causes of the Confederate Invasion of New Mexico." *New Mexico Historical Review* 8 (1933), 76–97.

Wilson, Spencer. "El Contadero." *Rio Grande History* 6 (1976), 6–7.

Wilson, Spencer and Robert A. Bieberman. "The Civil War in New Mexico: Tale Tales and True." In *Socorro Region II*, ed. Charles E. Chapin and Jonathan F. Callender. Thirty-fourth Field Conference, New Mexico Geological Society, Socorro, New Mexico (1983), 85–87.

Young, Bennett H. "Texas Cavalry Expedition in 1861–1862." *Confederate Veteran* 21 (March 1913), 16–19.

Zamonski, Stanley. "Colorado Gold and the Confederacy." In the 1956 Brand Book of the Denver Posse of The Westerners, ed. Numa L. James, 87–117. Boulder, CO: Johnson Publishing Co., 1957.

Miscellaneous

Abreu, Francisco. Letter to Major B. C. Cutler, dated June 27, 1865 (courtesy C. Meketa).

Andrews, Marshall. "Rates of Advance in Land Attack Against Unprepared Forces." Operations Research Office, Johns Hopkins University, 1960.

Berg, Richard. "Rio Grande—The Battle of Valverde, New Mexico Territory, February 21, 1862—A Richard Berg Game." *Strategy and Tactics* 143 (June 1991), 21–44 (plus attached game board).

Edrington, Thomas S. "The Confederate Victory at Pigeon's Ranch." Brochure published by General William R. Scurry Camp—Sons of Confederate Veterans, March 28, 1987.

Giese, Dale F. "Echoes of the Bugle." A Bicentennial Booklet published by Phelps-Dodge Corporation, 1976.

Helmbold, Robert L. "Rates of Advance in Historical Land Combat Operations." U.S. Army Concept Analysis Agency, Bethesda, Md., 1990.

Hunter, H. J. Miscellaneous Letters to Jettie Word (courtesy Jerry Thompson).

McCown, Captain J. B. Letter to *The Belleville Countryman*, Belleville, Texas, dated May 6, 1862 (courtesy Jerry Thompson).

Raguet Family Genealogy (unpublished; courtesy Jerry Thompson).

Scott, Charles R. Unpublished letter to Mr. C. A. Dupree, dated April 10, 1929 (courtesy S. A. Dupree).

Wallen, Major Henry D. "1862 Ammunition Inventory of Fort Union" (courtesy Charles Meketa).

Index

This index does not include individual entries for those men who are only listed as casualties in the Appendix. If one of the casualties is also referred to in the body of the text, he is included in the index. If an entry is italicized, it indicates that the reference to the individual or organization is on a figure, map, or photograph.